Charley Waterman's
TALES OF
FLY-FISHING,
WINGSHOOTING,
AND THE GREAT
OUTDOORS

Charley Waterman's
TALES OF
FLY-FISHING,
WINGSHOOTING,
AND THE GREAT
OUTDOORS

CHARLEY WATERMAN

THE DERRYDALE PRESS

Lanham • Boulder • New York • Toronto • Plymouth, UK

THE DERRYDALE PRESS

Published by The Derrydale Press
An imprint of Rowman & Littlefield
4501 Forbes Boulevard, Suite 200, Lanham, Maryland 20706
www.rowman.com

10 Thornbury Road, Plymouth PL6 7PP, United Kingdom

Distributed by National Book Network

British Library Cataloguing in Publication Information Available

Library of Congress Cataloging-in-Publication Data

The hardback edition of this book was previously cataloged by the Library of Congress as follows:

Waterman, Charles F.
Field days: irrepressible tales of fly fishing, wingshooting, and the great outdoors /
by Charley Waterman; foreword by Thomas McGuane; illustrations by Chuck Forman
p. cm.
1. Fly fishing—United States—Anecdotes. 2. Trout fishing—United States—
Anecdotes. 3. Fowling—United States—Anecdotes. 4. Outdoor recreation—
United States—Anecdotes. I. Title.
SK33.W295 1995
818'.5403—dc20
95-24135

Library of Congress Control Number: 2014936652
ISBN: 978-1-58667-132-7 (pbk : alk. paper)
ISBN: 978-1-58667-133-4 (electronic)

Printed in the United States of America

CONTENTS

FOREWORD

BY

THOMAS McGUANE

Writing about hunting and fishing is an old practice in America, partaking equally of logs, reports, adventurous accounts, and of course, tall tales. For the most part, its excuse for existing has been to offer practical advice. Its chronic weakness is that for a writer to consistently position himself to advise, he must be or pretend to be, an expert. In today's highly deteriorated situation, almost all we have are "experts" and our sporting literature reads like some obsessive *Consumer Reports* for outdoor gadgeteers. In sports like fly fishing and bird hunting, which appeal to either the literary or merely high falutin, the microscopic technical examination and mania for equipment has reached a point among the credulous as to drive sensible folk to catfish grappling, trotlining, or to the spotlighting of deer.

Charley Waterman has long since taken a bead on this problem. His broad focused knowledgeability is truly amazing; and he has left behind zones of expertise, like pistol shooting and sheep hunting, that even his fans have forgotten about. But he has never really set up as an expert. Like the great Havilah Babcock, his sense of humor is far too acute and perhaps not even under his own control, for him to work up the pompous tonalities that the sport gurus nowadays seem unable to do without.

He knows that if hunting and fishing are professionalized like everything else in this country, it's going to ruin them. At bottom, Charley Waterman is a midwesterner, a really pure one, with the region's genial impatience with bullshit. The great statement he makes about his beloved outdoors is the life he has committed to it. Probably the greatest stylistic accommodation he has made to changing times and an allowable gentrification has been to give up the single sighting plane of his accustomed over-and-under for a poetic little English double. Now that I've pointed this out, he'll start hankering for the Wingmasters at Kmart. Probably the weirdest thing I can imagine, is to address him as Charles. The last picture I saw of him with the English gun, he held it as though he had trained it to keep its distance.

Charley has been married these many years to Debie, the inventor of the hangy-downy fly; and it is to his everlasting credit that he has attempted to forge an identity of his own, without reference to the hangy-downy. I have been reading Charley for so long, and Debie is so embedded in my consciousness and everyone else's, as a character, that it is a pleasure to reminisce about them both as they have unfolded in Charley's writing, deep in secret beaver ponds prospecting for brook trout, catching plenty of fish by tried and true methods right among the tech-weenies of the spring creeks, or abroad on the vast sage-covered vacancies of public land looking for grouse. And I think of Charley best in our Western uplands, often with his old friend Ben Williams, behind Ben's battery of Brittanies, sometimes all pointing or backing at once like a bunch of iron filings around a magnet. What Charley stands for to another outdoorsman is life in the field, lived to the last drop.

I repeat that it is humor into which almost all is dissolved in Waterman's writings. At times you think of Mark Twain and even the great exaggerator, Petroleum V. Nasby. Frontier America produced a good many writers of high comic spirits; it seemed to go with finding the courage to enter new ground.

As a rural Kansan whose earliest fishing was on the water "tanks" or impoundments that served the solitary railroads, whose chain of title includes Civil War soldiers and one gunfighter, Charley Waterman has something of the frontier in him. It has to do with making do with what is at hand, rig something up that will work, and get out of the house. It is quite a different tradition than that which is evolving among the catalog sports of urban America, the spawn of hunting and fishing seminars or accelerated learning through videos. I do not believe Charley Waterman can be plunged into despair by low-modulus graphite, a fly sinking out of sight for lack of cul de canard, or the wrong choke tube on a wild flushing sharptail. He emerged in an era when we hadn't manipulated the hell out of the natural world, hadn't discovered fish scanners or GPS satellite locaters for the old whitetail stand. The venue of hunting and fishing was something you took neat; and often things went wrong but that's just how it went. It was the wild outdoors and if you minded your Ps and Qs, you might get to be a bit of veteran, know a thing or two, and be treated to the occasional success which in any case, was no occasion for crowing. There was a modesty appropriate to the awe of nature that made people hunt and fish in the first place.

Charley Waterman has written for a living for a very long time. This is a wretchedly hard thing for anyone to do. I am sure he has had occasions when a sustained meditation on a personal river or a courting of the soul through grouse hunting would have suited him fine. But a driving force in his hunt has been in bringing home the bacon. Therefore, a great portion of his body of work, like Red Smith's and Ring Lardner's, is in the form of short pieces, most often for magazines. But it is the steady accretion of sharp observation, common sense, amiable annoyance with pretense, and above all the homegrown speed of wit that unify his work and give it a natural wholeness.

I think of Charley Waterman as someone who knows where he stands. I remember running into him a quarter of a century ago right after he'd had his hair cut. Charley prefers a tonsorial style that suggests that he is being prepared for brain surgery. In those days, even the mildest bank vice president in the Northern Rockies sported pirate sideburns or a bandit moustache or a grand blow-dried pouf atop his pate, something to go with the Nehru suit in which he distributed ranch foreclosures.

"Charley," I asked, "are you trying to widen the generation gap?"

"No," he said, "I'm just trying to make it clear."

PREFACE

I never got paid for the first outdoor columns I wrote. I was a beat reporter on a newspaper and the managing editor said I could write the outdoor stuff only on my own time but that they would furnish the paper and typewriter ribbons. Of course, the editor did not know that I figured I was getting a big break, having wanted to be an outdoor writer since before I could spell it.

Since I got nothing for those early columns, I have long wondered if that was what they were worth. After I became the "outdoor writer" I was treated with suspicion by other members of the staff, and I have long suspected that the city editor was especially critical of anything I produced on other subjects.

This book is a collection of stuff I ran in various magazines. All of the stories are basically true. My wife, however, said recently that I tend to exaggerate. I told her that if I didn't exaggerate she'd be taking in washing.

It is stylish for outdoor writers to complain that the actual writing is pure drudgery and that they do it only so they can get out fishing or hunting. Since I am agreeably surprised that anyone wants to read my stuff, I'd just as soon write about hunting and fishing as be out doing it. However, if I didn't get out and do it, there would be nothing to write about. I could make all of it up, I suppose, but I am not that smart.

Anyway, I have been at this a long time and have known a lot of nice people in the process, and when I look at the makings of this book, I am shaken to see how many of the characters are now gone. This, I am told, is a negative approach to a foreword and won't sell books, but for that matter a lot of my characters do not have English shotguns and many use cheap fly reels. Most of my bird dogs have the champions a long way back in their lineage, and one of the best had no written pedigree at all. Neither do I.

But now and then I get a call or a letter from somebody I thought was a stranger a long way off who says he has read my stuff for forty years or so, and I guess that's what I'm after. If I retired, I'd do what I'm doing, only slower.

I went to a writer's seminar a while back and a nice lady asked me if I was planning to take up writing for a living. I have worried some about that.

Section One

FLY
FISHING

Chapter One

SISSY STICKS

My friend was standing in an anchored skiff in New Jersey's Barnegat Bay throwing streamers at striped bass. He had a nine-weight fly rod and was double hauling for distance. This was the kind of fishing he liked as he had been a pretty fair linebacker and athletic angling suited him fine.

A pair of fishermen idled past, watching with what appeared to be clinical interest. My friend decided to show off a little so he peeled off more line and fired a clean hundred feet—then pretended not to notice his gallery and waited to hear an admiring comment.

"Look at that!" said one of the observers, plainly audible over the outboard. "I'll bet that one wears silk underwear with lace."

That was years back and my sputtering friend survived. Only now are fly fishermen wading out from the general public's idea that they are a little strange. I recall when the editor of a very popular men's magazine was writing about the thrills of sports car driving and was extolling a particular model.

"This car is very easily handled," he said. "If you aren't man enough to drive it, you should take up fly fishing."

Back then, a bait fisherman asked me if I had been catching anything on my sissy stick. The effete label was partly dispelled by some prominent athletes of the time who became fly fishermen, and baseball's Ted Williams probably had the most effect of all. Jack Sharkey, former heavyweight champion of the world, also did some fly fishing, although some of his trout angling associates said he was a splashy wader.

Fly fishing has recently become an *in* thing, of course, but it still has its enemies, many of them impromptu critics who don't quite see how it works and aren't interested in that part. It has not been long since a guide I knew was driven out of a Yellowstone Park stream by disapproving spin fishermen. He had waded into a creek which was not yet mandatory catch-and-release and found the rainbows very willing to gulp dry flies of almost any pattern. He caught and released a number of them and had paid little attention to a gathering audience when trouble started.

On that particular day, hardware throwers weren't doing much good and some of them took exception to the "local" who kept catching and releasing fish—a procedure they felt was a demonstration of some sort of elitism and a subversion of the American way.

So the audience began to throw spoons at the wader while yelling that he should quit fooling around and let real fishermen fish. Until that time he had not realized releasing fish is sometimes considered a public insult. He had not been with me the day the tourist at a fishing pier told me he had seen someone "throwing back" fish and wanted to know whom to report it to.

For a long time in many areas (and in a few today), the completely equipped fly fisherman's costume has made him a comic character. Although waders, vest, and assorted dangling gadgets are worn proudly (and often expensively) in many

4

circles, they stir the juices of professional newspaper and magazine cartoonists. Lately the fly person's equipment has become a little dressier and more expensive than the nearly forgotten Dacron leisure suit. For years I have bored my friends with the tale of Fred Terwilliger and me meeting mounted Argentinean gauchos in the moonlight when we were wearing waders and everything that went with them. The gauchos' huge black dogs bawled fearsomely. The resultant rodeo was happily masked by dust and darkness but I have no doubt the gauchos are still telling the story.

Although I may have been called strange names by many who have seen me wading small streams, it is in outboard boating areas that yesterday's fly rodder was most likely to hear the public's opinion of him. Few of its users know that the things they say loudly over an outboard's mutter can be heard for some distance.

In the South, when wading and casting flies for shad, I had heard innumerable derogatory comments, but I was surprised to hear from a big outboard cruiser the following:

"Look at that damned tourist with the fly pole. Watch me gun this hooker and fill his rubber pants full of water!"

That's what he did. In most parts of the U.S., even those largely dependent upon tourist trade, the word "tourist" has generally been derogatory when used by locals. Even if you have grown old but a few miles from where you are throwing a fly, you'll hear things like:

"Lookit the tourist with the fly rig after bream. I wonder what he'd do if an ol' bass grabbed that thing!"

In recent years the routine landing of hundred-pound saltwater fish by fly casters has gradually changed the perception of other anglers, but a few years back I was interrupted while talking about snook at a tackle counter.

A bystander walked up to the counter, leaned around so that he could look me in the face and stated:

"Nobody can catch a snook on a fly rod!"

Such places are pretty scarce now, but until recent years there were quite a few resort operators who did not understand that fly fishermen had not turned to the method as a last resort. I wanted to go back to a Colorado resort and called to ask about the fishing. The owner said the fishing was great and I arrived there in a hurry, tired and sleepy, and he met me with enthusiasm.

"I wanted to surprise you," he said. "The river's so high and muddy you don't even have to use flies. You can catch 'em on worms!"

Please don't repeat this, but there are certain times and places when other artificial methods are better than flies. Some fly fishing converts take great effort to level this off and I have read complete books on ways of slinging all sorts of weighted lures with fly rods. These lures range from plugs that would work fine on spinning gear to deep-going flies with heavy sinkers. There was the backcountry bass fisherman who put a big live shiner on a fly rod, lowered it into a desirable spot, rowed seventy-five feet away, dropped his anchor, and waited for action. He said he couldn't cast the bait with his fly rod but he was fly fishing.

Of course for a very long time anglers have trolled with fly rods for landlocked salmon, using canoes, and it was accepted as a sporting method. Only a few years back, I knew some trollers who caught shad on fly rods, and there was a special method in that madness—the gentle nodding of the long rods gave the tiny lures an action the shad loved, but now most trollers use soft spinning rods.

I don't know if "yuppie" is complimentary or derogatory but it is often applied to fly fishermen. I didn't know how far I had strayed until I met an angler who had read some of the things I had written.

"Oh, I know who you are!" he said with a recognition that made me feel warm all over. "You're the guy who writes all of those articles with pictures of somebody in greasy jeans landing a fish on a fly rod!"

After that, I got some nice duck pants and some of those shirts with special ventilation gussets and my wife bought me a new fishing vest with red pockets. I also took a little more interest in my tackle. Oh, I'd spent more than I could afford on rods before that, but I had been a little careless about my reels. I had good, big reels that would handle almost anything I could get hold of, and I put about the same ones on most of the rods, but I saw the big reels made my fish look smaller in pictures so I got some little shiny ones.

In country where there weren't many fly fishermen, I learned long ago to ignore comments from others. I am not as quick on the trigger as my old friend who used to play tackle for a pretty good university football team and appears rather large at his upper end. He slid into a cove in his floater bubble and began to cast over clean trout water, ten feet deep. There was a boat and two fishermen already in the little cove and one of them told him they were there first and he was taking away their privacy.

"Mister," said John, "you probably think I am floating in this thing, but I'm not. I'm standing on the bottom."

There are compensations for all the fly fishing indignities I have suffered through the years. A while back I was wading along a black bass shoreline, throwing a bug at lily pads and over some eelgrass. A young couple came sliding past with an electric motor on a bass boat. They had spinning rods. The lady was pretty.

"Gee," she said, "look at the way that line curls out there. That's pretty. I didn't know they could do that! Why don't we learn to fish that way?"

Aw, shucks, ma'am. Nothin' to it.

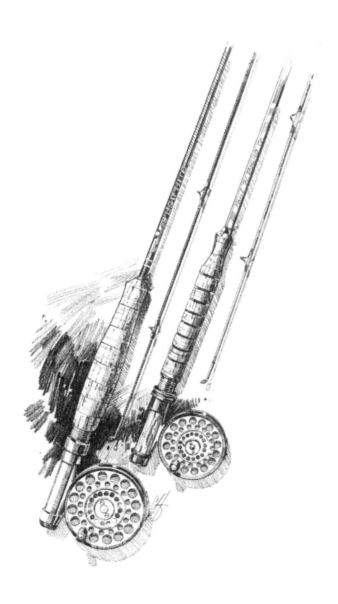

Chapter Two

FANATICS AND
FLY POLES

Once while writing a book about the development of American angling, and feeling very professional, I contacted an expert on the history of fly rods to get the inside track on that business. It was a hobby of hers so the historian was eager to give me a little inside dope for a very reasonable price.

I had no idea of what I was getting into, and just now I was about to say I opened a real can of worms, but the mention of canned worms in a dissertation of this sort would be very bad form. Let's say I opened a real can of nymphs. After a few days I found it necessary to curb the historian's enthusiasm, even though I was getting a little hooked on the subject myself. I told the lady that it was going to be only an average-sized book and while it was good to say just who made the first split-bamboo fly rod and where, I did not think it necessary to find the exact spot where he stood or where he threw the chips.

The rod is the major unit of the fly fisherman's outfit, but it is now losing some of its glamour because the latest graphites (said by many to be the greatest rods ever) can be turned out in practically duplicate form. Up until glass and carbon materials came along, no two fine rods were exactly alike in action, and owners of truly fine bamboos were generally prosperous types who smoked bent pipes and wore tweed jackets.

However, some of the most carefully built bamboos weren't especially good and there were some veteran anglers who had some very strange and very expensive ones. Most of them were made to order but came from such weird ideas and had such bad casting forms that the results were pretty useless, buggy whips no longer being big sellers. Some of the things had famous names because the makers were willing to turn a quick buck, even if they winced. All of these rods had pretty silk wrappings and still remind me of those very expensive watches that have no numbers on their faces. But other famous bamboo whittlers were so firm in their beliefs about rods that they made all of them to suit themselves and, if you didn't like it, you could go to hell.

For a long time glue was a big problem with split cane and I knew a national casting champion who made his own rods—and in a hurry. The strips tended to come apart and the sticks looked as if they were selected from a trash pile, but when he won tournaments no one noticed the rods had cracks.

Before this splitting business got started, woods with fancy names were chased all over the world. After Samuel Phillippi of Easton, Pennsylvania, really started the "rent-and-glue" number, we didn't hear much about mahoe from Cuba or bethabara and snakewood from the Guianas.

My old bass bug rod, which I was using in 1934, looks like later ones but is a little soft. I thought it was a real powerhouse when I got it but I later decided it was a little floppy. Chuck Schilling, a well-known tackle manfacturers' rep for many years and a student of rods, straightened me out on that.

"Back then most of those fly casters threw bait, too," he said. "They didn't want a fast rod to ruin their crawdads."

When I got that first good cane rod, I was enchanted by the beautiful grain and the gleaming varnish, but an old-timer I knew had a rod with a lot of really pretty silk wrappings. They were in tastefully varied colors and went from end to end, whereas my treasure had only dark red wrappings at the guides and ferrules. I fished with this veteran, who was careful not to note the inferiority of my equipment. I considered having someone do a more colorful thread number on my bug rod, so I visited a tackle expert.

"The reason his stick has thread all over it is that the damned thing's got a lousy glue job and is apt to fly apart without a dozen spools of wrapping," the expert pronounced. "I don't care how much he paid for it. All that string screws up the action."

Fly rods are a good tool for expressing your individuality. Although wire "snake" guides are accepted as the logical route for expensive lines, I knew a bass fisherman who said they looked cheap and didn't shoot line very well. So he had agate guides from butt to tip. Agate, of course, was the chosen material for good baitcasting rods, but when you had nine feet of them on a fly rod, the unit performed much like a cow whip and the overweighted tip sagged a foot when the rig was resting. He learned to cast with it because a man has his pride. After a few years of that he could have taken up professional arm wrestling.

But pretty wrappings have been important, and when some Oriental copies appeared long ago they were marvels of artistic expression. There was a little problem with these rods, however, in that the makers didn't know what a fly rod is used for. My friend ordered one through the captain of a freight airline and was dazzled by its beauty fresh from the package—but some of the better rake handles were more efficient casting devices. The last he saw of it a kid was rolling a tin can with it. But then, you can buy artistic Chinese guns that were never made to shoot.

There have been really fine bamboo fly rods around for many years, of course, and some of the old ones are worth considerable cash. I shall not name any of them lest heirs to trunkfuls of rent-and-glued cane rush to the publisher and demand price estimates. Since I once told a man his inherited rod was worth about $30 and found I was $2,000 off, I have been hesitant to discuss such things.

Of course the real mystery of this business is that nobody can tell you exactly why such-and-such a rod is highly valued by all sorts of men in tweed jackets. Generally, it's a famous name and the catch is that a rod one caster loves will help another caster strangle himself in fly line. I fish with a fine caster who has a valuable Payne, but he uses it only on nice days with no wind and no brush along the creek—and there is always the possibility of rod bandits. I have nightmares about backing the truck over it.

There was a time when tiny rods, especially short ones, were accepted as a badge of expertise. I guess the late Lee Wulff did more than anyone else to make these fragile wands prestigious. Someone came up with the name "flea rod" and good bamboo went into little things five or six feet long for everything from bluegills to sailfish. Lee Wulff never said his little rods were more efficient. He just showed he could do a good job of casting and playing fish with them. Like a few others who practiced, he could throw a pretty good line with his bare hands.

When glass rods began to take over from some of the less expensive canes, we had some unique experiences and some of the old-timers said glass would go the way of hollow steel, which didn't last too long but made a strong move in the thirties. At one time, you know, they used to put steel cores in split-bamboo rods to make them stronger. This did not contribute much to the action. There was a period when an occasional glass rod would sort of explode in your hand as everything gave way at once. It was more interesting when some of the first graphites blew up, but nobody got hurt that I know of.

With the new materials, there were guys in eyeshades and white jackets who thought up some peachy ideas. One was that you really needed only one rod for everything—marlin to bluegills. You just built a nice, long glass rod with a stiff butt that would hardly bend at all, a middle section that worked some, and a flippy, dippy tip that would wave in a light breeze. It was concluded that if you had the wrong timing for one section of the rod, there would be another part that would take up the slack and work for you. It turned out to be a lousy rod, but it sold pretty well, and if you used one the old-timers would stop fishing and watch you with their mouths open. I have always felt that did a great deal to encourage baitfishing with cane poles.

Now the graphite rod business sneaked up on a lot of us who didn't know what graphite was. Grabbing for business, those who sold the new rods came up with a lot of words I didn't understand—words right out of the lab where those guys in the white jackets were mixing stuff. "Modulus" came along with a lot of figures and there was a question of whether you wanted "high" modulus or "low" modulus. As I recall, there was little discussion of "medium" modulus, but I knew right away that all of those rods had modulus.

Graphite had the stuff all right, and when a fly-fishing instructor I knew worked a youth camp it turned out that the kids, displaying the spooky coordination that some teenagers have, chose graphite rods over both cane and glass. They were not dazzled by knowing someone had whittled, glued, and varnished cane that had been cut in a corner of Asia where the temperature and rainfall are just right.

Since graphite works so well and is so easy on your arm, it was natural for somebody to figure ten-foot graphite rods would be better than short ones, and almost suddenly we had a brand new cult.

Now ten-foot trout rods were nothing new, but I thought they had slipped off into the past along with gut leaders and solid-wood fly poles made of lumber from strange countries with long names. The traditional two-handed split-bamboo salmon rods, especially those favored by the English, had been around almost since the beginning of cane splitting.

I saw an English visitor operate with a fourteen-foot salmon rod in our salt water and he did pretty well with it. At the time, I had never heard of "spey casting." In tournament cast ing, the two-handed-rod distance event required a very long rig, and to win that event you had to throw a shooting head out of sight, but I never saw any of those outfits used on sunfish or crappie.

When light, powerful graphite came along, a ten-foot rod didn't feel heavy at all in one hand and a bunch of missionaries began to demonstrate ten-footers everywhere they could get someone to watch. They worked fine and people who had forgotten what color their backing was found they could throw off the whole 100-foot-and-something line without a running start. Except that they had to be taken down to fit in a station wagon and stuck out too far from small boats, the ten-footers were fine. Believers in long rods demonstrated how they could keep the line working above the brush along many trout streams, and except that they were easily broken by absent-minded passersby and were frequently caught in doors, no one came up with other disadvantages. If it was too long to handle a fish you could just dip the tip a little so he wouldn't have so much leverage.

But extra-long rods are not very popular anymore, even though they sold well for a while. And I don't know what I did with my six-footers. If you think of something else that might catch on for a while, let me know and we'll sell it.

Along with graphite, a wide variety of specialized fly lines, and light shooting-line material, we are getting some pretty fancy figures in the record books. Phillip C. Miraville and Jim Green of the Golden Gate Casting Club at San Francisco inaugurated monofilament as shooting line in 1946 and when Green threw 149 feet at the next national tournament, the other casters complained bitterly and began to use mono themselves. Since then, we've had better lines, and graphite came along to fire casts farther than bamboo or glass ever had. Just recently Steve Rajeff threw more than 230 feet with a one-handed fly rod, a discouraging event to those who had hoped some day to reach a hundred while fishing. Oh, that's specialized tackle all right but it's worth noticing.

But I'll never get over the split-cane business, I guess, and I know a few diehards who use it for light fishing, even though they go to graphite for the heavy stuff. Bamboo rods are still being made, largely for connoisseurs, or for those who would like to be connoisseurs, and some of the old names are still with us. The Winston bamboo rod gained much of its fame in tournaments of many years ago and I have met some of those who actually made the early ones, and others who built the modern versions that go along with topnotch graphite ones. Although their talk of how rods are made goes mostly over my head, there is one phase that I understand.

A "modern" Winston expert said that when a bamboo rod is finished (generally with two tips) they take it out and cast with it to be sure everything is right. And he admitted the two tips wouldn't work exactly the same but that now and then there'd be a combination that all of the workers knew was as near perfect as a rod could be .

The workmen there have always been fishermen and I have always wondered if all those "perfect" rods were ever shipped.

Chapter Three

How to be a Famous Fisherman

Ｉf you want to be a Famous Fisherman I can help you. I have been watching people become Famous Fishermen since before lipped plugs became crankbaits.

During that period I was more interested in becoming a Famous Writer than a Famous Fisherman, but I did so poorly that I see now I should have taken the other route. It is a little late for me but you probably have time.

There are several procedures that will make you a Famous Fisherman, and I shall take them up one by one. Most winners have used them all and may have followed some plans I don't know about.

First, you must keep telling people you are a Famous Fisherman. Can you think of any Famous Fisherman who has not written about it or appeared on TV programs? Many folks have the false impression that a fisherman first becomes a master technician and then writes about it. The true angling celebrity writes about it while he is learning. He hopes that by the time he has convinced people he is an expert, he will be.

I was in a tackle shop when a young fellow came in and told the proprietor that he was a fishing celebrity. Those were the exact words he used, and I felt very cheap that I had not heard of him. He sold the store some of his books on fishing. The spelling was not too good, but I understand he became a successful guide. The book had only 140 pages, but you had to read it kind of slow.

If you want to be a Famous Fisherman but can barely write home for money, don't worry about it. There are establishments called "vanity publishers" who will publish anything, even if they can't tell what it is about, as long as you pay them. And to be famous you don't need to sell very many books. Some of the most valued fishing volumes in the world are collector's items because there weren't very many of them printed and they got scarce fast. They're first editions all right. In many cases the author carried the whole edition home with him under one arm. Many of these treasures wouldn't pass a seventh-grade composition assignment. A leather binding is a help, since everyone knows that anything bound in leather is literary.

If you write about fishing, be sure to have some pictures of big fish. It is relatively simple to do this, and mounted specimens work fine as long as you throw them slightly out of focus. In telling anecdotes about fishing, always explain that such-and-such happened while you were instructing so-and-so in a special fishing method.

It is not necessary to have a really special method, but a special name for it is essential. I think the term "doodlesocking" is one of the best examples of that. It was recently applied to an ancient method of bass fishing involving heavy-handed operation of a canepole. If you write about bass fishing, for example, I think "boomershooting" is a good term that has not yet been used and could be applied to all sorts of angling operations.

My wife and I starred in a couple of television angling movies, one of which involved snook and tarpon fishing. The best scene showed Debie (pronounced *Deebee*) playing a tarpon that jumped all over a bay but the boys in the cutting room had her landing a snook. Since neither of the people who saw this movie called about the goof, I submit it as proof that you needn't be too meticulous about such things. Debie and I never were in enough television to become Famous Fisherpersons. I suspect the fact that Debie fell in while wading with an expensive microphone fastened to her shirt may have gotten us blackballed.

Whether in print, on TV, or in personal conversation, it is essential that a Famous Fisherman familiarize himself with true piscatorial language, and in this geography and method are all-important. For example, freshwater trout fishermen north of Tennessee speak considerable Latin, and black bass fishermen south of there are careful to conceal any implication of literacy.

A famous fly caster in Pennsylvania is likely to point out that his fly imitates the *Pseudocloeon anoka* dun, thus establishing himself a notch above anyone who calls the same creature a brownish bug. In Georgia, a shiner soaker who mentioned that his bait is a member of the family *Cyprinidae* would probably be buying his own beer for some time. A famous trout angler, of course, should not be interested in beer and is likely to drink wine from a *bota*, a kind of waterproof leather sack with a squirt nozzle on it that allows you to drink like a chicken, by tilting your head back. If appearance is the only important thing, of course, you could put beer or Classic Coke in your bota and no observer would know. If your bota is really made of leather, you probably couldn't tell the difference either.

The terminology of North and South is deeply divided. For example, no true southern bassin' man will call a big bass a bass if he can remember to call it a "sow" or a "hawg." And in the North a trout angler would say a fish produced a slash rise. He would never say it splashed like hell.

It is very difficult for an English professor to become a famous bass fisherman for he has difficulty in leaving off his "g's," no matter how far he spits or how many plastic worm ads he paints on his boat. However, it has been done by a few who could go from the lily pads to the classroom without so much as a split infinitive.

TV fishing ordinarily demands dialogue, although I feel there are times when tense silence would be better. As in any other form of communication there have been some sparkling phrases—so colorful they are repeated over and over on the air. These include:

"Man, he sure is a fighter!"

"Yourn is biggerin' mine!"

"Boy, oh boy!"

"Lookit 'im go!"

"Gol Dang!"

"I love it!"

It is necessary for some of these phrases to be repeated as reruns, so to speak, because some of the writers of fishing-show copy have abandoned the field and now are writing dialogue for professional wrestling interviews.

In becoming a Famous Fisherman it is essential that you do something unique. For example, I once achieved local fame as a black bass angler by catching fish on crochet thread. I am modest about this achievement, partly because the thread tested twenty-eight pounds, but I feel this area could be further explored. When spinning tackle was new, I was acquainted with an offshore angler who became temporarily famous by catching sailfish on spinning gear. This technique involved a special form of skill because he could not get much of his eighty-pound monofilament on the reel.

Many years ago a really good Florida fisherman became a Famous Fisherman by catching alligators on a fly rod. This was a surprise to him, I think, but a New York columnist happened to see him do it, and the farther away a reader gets from alligators, the harder they are to catch on a fly rod. They were not very big alligators.

Along this line, I note that hardly anyone has done much fishing in the Gulf Stream with a belly boat or float tube. This is a wide-open field, and if you have no float tube, you can make one from an old truck innertube.

There are essential words. The term "structure" is a rather recent addition to fishing literature and is used by famous bass fishermen to describe almost anything beneath the surface. For example, if a bass fisherman looks over the side in clear water and sees a diesel locomotive down there, he probably will state that it is structure. If it were running, I still doubt that he would call it a diesel locomotive. You don't mention specific names where "structure" will cover the subject. Even saltwater fishermen have discovered this word, and if lost Atlantis is ever located offshore I'm sure it will be described as structure.

By now you may realize that a Famous Fisherman must resign himself to a sort of restrictive popularity. I doubt if one can ever be recognized in all schools of sport fishing. For example, Roland Martin was unknown at a big Trout Unlimited meeting where I held an inquiry, and some bassers thought Douglas Swisher was a tight end. I was able to convince both groups that Kip Farrington was a rock star. If none of these names mean anything to you, it is probably just as well. Potential Famous Fishermen should never recognize established Famous Fishermen except when engaged in name-dropping.

In dropping a name, never allow it to appear that the owner of the dropped name taught you anything or was in any way your superior in any area. You can always say that such-and-such happened when so-and-so (a Famous Fisherman) was just getting started or was visiting you to learn more about sheefish or steelhead. Keep showing up at fishing resorts and inquiring if such and such a Famous Fisherman is around. Leave your name for him to call you and mumble that "the jerk is late again."

Catching record fish is a good way to get started toward fame, but it is a little difficult to break into some categories. For example, it might take quite a while to catch the biggest fly-rod tarpon with people like Billy Pate around. However, there are some wide-open categories. For example, I have never heard of anyone claiming a two-pound line record for the shovelnose guitarfish. The drill is to catch one, declare a record, and produce considerable information about what a hell-slather fighter the shovelnose guitarfish is. The International Game Fish Association is making this sort of practice easier by offering to recognize some new record species like the leatherskin queenfish.

One step toward fame is the use of a unique boat, especially one with a colorful name. I very nearly made it once when I was invited to speak at an angler's club because the program chairman thought I was the owner of a boat with a risqué name. He was disappointed when I said I had no boat with a dirty name, for he'd supposed I was quite a card. To get this kind of start, all you need is a little paint and a brush. Everybody knows the owner of a boat with a dirty name is a fun guy.

Put your own name on your boat—something like "Joe Blow, Master Of Angling" or "Joe Blow, World Champion Fisherman." There once was a casting champion from Chicago who wore white shirts with "World Champion Fisherman" across the shoulders in letters three inches high. That was in a day before coveralls with short sleeves were called jumpsuits, and most of those who saw those shirts thought it was a gag, even though the man had the trophies to prove he was a world champion—at least in casting.

The word "champion" though is very important, and I suspect that almost everyone is a champion at something if he will just find out what. That shovelnose guitarfish, for example, could make you a world champion in a hurry, and there might not be a runner-up.

At one time, all famous male fishermen smoked pipes when being photographed and did so even if pipe smoking made them deathly ill. The Old Hat custom prevails in some areas. Famous Fishermen were supposed to wear old and filthy hats and their wives were supposed to be continually endeavoring to capture the hats and throw them away. The Old Hat custom is fading a little after a hundred years. Bass fishermen, however, have gone to visor caps with advertising. Nothing makes quite the impression of a bright orange cap advertising Glutz Worms or the like. This advertising theme can be carried over into jumpsuits, the implication being that somebody paid for use of the space, even if the jumpsuit wearer bought the patches himself. Remember, we are not into the financial end at the moment, only building an image we might cash in on later.

All Famous Fishermen are supposed to be widely traveled, and it is a rule that the farther away fish are, the larger they become. The principle of distance adding prestige is applied to anglers seeking recognition far from home as well as to those making long trips to inform the home folks.

Some time back I received a call from a touring angler who wanted to know where he could catch large bass. He explained that he was not interested in six- and eight-pound bass, as he could catch all of those he wanted back home. This interested me, as I have never been able to catch all of the six- and eight-pound bass I wanted and have tried for some time. I asked him where he lived, and he said he came from Missouri. Since I have fished some in Missouri and have found some days when I was a little short of six- and eight-pound bass, I realized that I was dealing with a Famous Fisherman in the making. I said that I knew just how he felt, as I had fished in Missouri and realized that six- and eight-pound bass could get very tiresome. For a moment I thought the phone had gone dead, but he recovered quickly and requested the location of some "ten- and twelve-pound bass." I told him where they were but did not mention that I hadn't caught a ten-pound bass in sixteen years. I think he thinks I am a Famous Fisherman.

Famous Fishermen continually report how they solved an angling mystery after everyone else had given up. It is essential, however, that this be done with a flair and described in proper terminology. I feel that Harry Murray, who has a tackle shop in Virginia, accomplished this when he was a youth and did it to perfection.

I must mention for you unlettered types that "matching the hatch" is a term used in high-class trout circles when you find an artificial fly that matches the real ones the fish are pigging out on. Harry used that term, although his stroke of genius had nothing to do with trout. It seems Harry fished a small

Virginia stream that had chicken hatcheries along its banks, and when hatching eggs went bad the operators would throw them into the creek. In Virginia and points north there is a rather uncivilized fish called a fallfish, with a reputation roughly equivalent to Louisiana mudfish. Fallfish along Harry's creek became hooked on chicken eggs, so to speak, and watchful Harry made some lures to match them. Having a lot of class, Harry said he was "matching the hatch."

One sure ploy in the business of fame is growing older, actually a rather simple process. Speaking of the "old days" sets one apart from johnny-come-lately fishermen, no matter how advanced or scientific their methods. It is widely known that the old days were much better, having more and larger fish.

An important feature of the old days is that the older the days, the less accurate need be reports concerning them. I find that in order to handle this properly, certain evidence must be tactfully destroyed. I recently burned a quantity of photographs made many years ago, all of them showing fish that were incredibly small, and although I feel this was largely caused by some shrinking of the photographic emulsion itself, I saw no reason to leave such spurious documentation around. Although I have long since abandoned any thought of being a Famous Fisherman, I felt the record should be left open, so to speak, and unencumbered by questionable photographs.

Chapter Four

FUZZ AND FEATHERS

Even though all red-blooded outdoorsmen remember it, let's review the story about how a breathless world learned that deer hair is a deadly lure for game fish.

It seems a hunter wearing a coonskin cap and carrying a muzzleloader shot a deer on the bank of a stream and as he started to drag it away from the edge, a little ball of hair blew into the water. All of the civilized world knows that a big largemouth bass banged the surface to a haze and clobbered the bit of fluff. The exact location of this breakthrough remains a bit obscured by the mists of time, and I have heard rumors that it was a northern pike instead of a bass, but I have no doubt that the story is basically true, as no one has ever flatly disputed it.

There is another pretty good story about the Washington kid chopping down a fruit tree, but it has no relation to fly fishing and I feel it is superfluous to repeat it.

Since fly fishing is an intellectual pursuit involving the depths of both art and science, the means by which flies (this includes streamers and floating bugs) are constructed should be of vital interest to all real fishermen. Izaak Walton, who recorded some early fishing activities, termed his fishing friends "brothers of the angle." This is a very perceptive term because there are more angles to fly fishing than to any other outdoor pursuit I have read about.

Although those early fly fishermen used a variety of materials in the construction of their best flies, none of them has made any mention of Pogo hair, which indicates that we have progressed considerably since then. Pogo hair proved highly effective for some time with streamer flies used for smallmouth bass in Ozark streams. When Pogo died, he left quite a gap in the list of topnotch fly-tying materials.

Pogo was a large, sort of cream-white dog belonging to Buddy Nordmann, an old fishing friend of mine. Further description of Pogo is rather complex since it is customary to say a particular dog is long-haired or short-haired. Pogo was partly long-haired and partly short-haired as he was frequently clipped in sections as desired for various streamers or bugs. Pogo's hair was a pretty good substitute for polar bear hair, which is a favorite of experienced fishermen and can be a little expensive whenever polar bears are scarce. There was no charge for Pogo's hair, although he became increasingly hard to catch as the value of his plumage became better known. With his passing the "brothers of the angle" lost a valued associate.

Generally fly-tying materials are more expensive when they come from a great distance, as from India or Yemen. This condition has often become complicated by the fact that the importation of various kinds of feathers and fur has been disapproved by border officials who might miss a traveling shipment of cocaine but are deadly at collaring packages of exotic duck feathers. Lately the restrictions have been lifted slightly but there is no telling when there may be new clampdowns, which undoubtedly leads to clandestine hoarding by fly tyers.

There are famous fly tyers with world-wide reputations, but whomping up a streamer or dry fly can be learned by most persons with self-control, iron nerves, and determination. Even I have produced some bass streamers. Hence, one of the attractions of fly fishing is that the fisherman can make his own flies much easier than he could design plugs or spoons.

He can also (and this is important) give these flies his own name, which adds greatly to his self-esteem. Then too, he can tie famous patterns just a little different and give them new names as well. Of course, if the original name is catchy, it can be used for anything that faintly resembles it.

Take Lefty's Deceiver, which was put together by Lefty Kreh. I do not remember what the original looked like, but a generation-and-a-half of fly tyers have produced things they called Lefty's Deceiver, some of which would be a considerable surprise to Lefty, especially if he met them in subdued light. I think the only requirement for the name "Lefty's Deceiver" is that the tyer be thinking of Lefty Kreh while he is tying it.

Poultry has become rather expensive but the birds that produce feather "necks" for fly tyers are out of the Kentucky Fried Chicken class. I see in a catalog here that a "Super Grizzly Neck" (having nothing to do with bears but involving the skin from part of a bird's forward section) will cost you around sixty dollars. After those feathers are gone, I have long wondered if the rest of the chicken is good to eat.

Now "jungle cock eyes" have nothing to do with an exotic bird's vision, but are feathers with a design that looks as if they are watching you when they are tied into a streamer. They cost fifty cents apiece or better, are very popular for really big attractors, and the bird can keep producing them as long as he feels like it. They're imported and for a time it was illegal to bring them in, which led to introduction of Mylar "jungle cock eyes" at a little more than a nickel apiece. Deer hair is relatively inexpensive and a deerhair bug floats well since the hairs are hollow.

The deerhair floating "mouse" is shaped the way it sounds and has been shaped the way it sounds ever since the buckskinner whacked the deer. Some fly tyers can put the stuff together so tightly that the ends of the hairs make the whole thing almost smooth. I knew a fly manufacturer who produced some of those things that were a big hit with the customers, even having eyes (up on top where the bass couldn't see them) and sometimes tails. After I knew him for a while, he told me not to use those pretty ones and gave me some shaggy things that appeared to have been tied by beginners, and most of them had been. They looked like mice that had gone through a vacuum sweeper, and that was what the bass went for. He said the best fish-catchers wouldn't sell so he gave them to his friends.

Long ago I bought a synthetic mouse. It was white with leather ears, a leather tail, and beady eyes. It sank immediately. Some realistic mice today cost ten bucks apiece.

The word "fly" has been used rather loosely and some of the folks who wouldn't fish with anything but a fly rod have cast everything from plastic worms to little leather alligators, eventually graduating to shotputting or discus throwing. I am reminded of the elongated artificial-hair streamers that do so well on barracuda and some other saltwater fish. They were first made from what we called "doll hair," and some of the streamers are a foot long or longer, competing with the surgical tubing thrown with spinning, plugging, and surf rods.

I think I know who invented the hair apparatus, which doesn't really cast all that badly with a heavy rod, but some day I hope to hold a reunion of all of the fishermen who claim to have introduced the thing. It will be a sort of who's who of heavy fly fishing, and there should be some very interesting characters.

It was a pan fisherman who challenged Pogo and the polar bears for supremacy in the softish, whitish stuff for small flies. He found that if you stripped the rubber coating off some kinds of electric cord, there was some soft, cottony stuff over the wire and he tied it on some small hooks for the undoing of countless crappie and bluegills. He was one of those guys who wanted to reinvent everything himself, regardless of expense and trouble. I worried about power outages.

Some years back, there was something known in tying circles as The Great Mylar Massacre. It was found that shiny strips of Mylar could be used to add flash to a streamer, and since Mylar was used for a variety of things such as waving in the wind at used-car lots, there were shifty-eyed fly tyers slinking through many of the halls of commerce. It was found that the wider strips of material cast like open umbrellas, so there were all sorts of methods of getting really fine, shiny strips.

The ever-watchful purveyors of fly-tying materials leaped into the breach and brought out all colors of shiny strips of the right width under several trade names.

One of the later innovations is bugs cut out of the soles of department store flip-flops. The soles are made up of different colors of soft plastic, and a friend of mine rigged a thing that took out bug-shaped cores when used like a doughnut cutter. They sure caught bass, although I doubt if they were better than commercial products. He wasn't trying to save money, but a man has his pride.

There was, of course, the bug that wound up a rubber band while being cast and swam about on its own after it hit the water. The inventor said it never caught many fish, but it sure was fun to use. When cast, it sounded a little like a low-level strafing attack.

A friend of mine is one of the world's best fly fishermen and will not use any fly or bug he hasn't constructed himself. Give him a type of fly that is working particularly well and he won't use it today, but he'll have one just like it tomorrow. I have often wondered what he did with the ones he copied.

Another friend was intrigued by a particular streamer with a red-feather tail. He'd buy the streamer but he always cut off a quarter-inch of the tail. Nobody was going to make a conformist out of him!

Chapter Five

DEBIE
POPPERS

The best of our Kansas fly fishing was in the tank ponds (sometimes called railroad ponds) that were formed by combination dams and railroad grades. Steam locomotives still needed water to pull grain, coal, and passengers across a thousand railway spurs to a thousand tank towns that had sprouted where the water tanks stood.

For me and the other bug casters in 1934 the best fishing nearly always came on sultry summer evenings when wading fishermen were footnotes to gigantic thunderheads and crows were headed to roost. There was a coyote song now and then and often the drone of a Fordson tractor as a tired farmer worked late.

Farlington Pond was reed rimmed and full of vegetation, some of it rotted and making a soft bottom that smelled of decay when stirred up. Sometimes we waded deep and I even did a little awkward swimming in deep spots, trying to keep my precious fly rod dry. It was good bamboo and I still have it.

Rainbow trout were clear over in Missouri. Our best bugs were the Buckhair Floater and the Dragon Fly.

At Russell Francis's Fly Shop, where he produced flies for Midwestern dealers, some of them in large towns I had never seen, beginners made the best Buckhair Floaters. Experienced fly makers let their pride get in the way and turned out beautiful, tightly tied "powderpuffs" or "hair mice," but since largemouth black bass seem to have little appreciation of artistic form, the added attraction of ragged hair ends simply caught more fish, and still does.

Some of the best bugs were hard to cast with those bamboo rods that would work with what we'd call eight-weight lines today. I once wrote that the Dragon Fly cast like a readymade bow tie. It was an elongated cork body with a flat nose and a sprig of deerhair tail. The hair wings were set at a right angle to the body. If it wanted to twist in the air and the gut leader wasn't quite stiff enough to prevent that, the Dragon Fly would have things pretty well wound up when it hit the water. Let it lie for a moment and the leader would begin to untwist, the bug doing a series of slow barrel rolls, apparently under its own power. Although real dragon flies never looked or acted like that, the combination proved infuriating to a lot of bass. Although I have studied the rise forms of snobbish trout on both paper and water, I have a special thing for a bass taking a popping bug.

Black bass strikes and bombing runs have been described in similar terms for so many years that an analysis may seem anticlimactic. The hard take throws water and makes a startling chug (accepted term for this is "explosion")—produced by a bass intending to kill something he means to eat or smash because he is in a bad humor. Although many fish are caught in these long-remembered charges, any live target making as much fuss as a hard-worked popper would weigh so much it couldn't just ride the bow wave to safety. The problem here is dramatized by trying to grab a bug by hand from underneath when it is floating in a wash basin. Then there are the slurp strikes and the ones in which the bass simply opens his mouth and closes it silently over the bug. "Ominous" is the traditional term for any slow approach by a bass.

The Stunted Skunk was a monster built to compete with the loudest plugs thrown by baitcasters. Its nose was ⅞-inch across and its hair was black except for the white back stripe. "Popper" is too delicate a name for such a tool. Many years later my wife Debie designed the Debie Popper, simply an elongated bug with a very cheap and light wire hook. It sat high and hopped about happily, catching both freshwater and saltwater fish, but it would be no good for commercial production since the flimsy hook simply rusted away, and it was the light hook that let it skip.

Bass bugs may lack the glamour of delicate trout flies or ornate salmon creations but I began with them and am sentimental about the places they have taken me.

In the Ozark mountain streams (most of them now irregular "structure" on the bottoms of great impoundments), the smallmouths came in bronze flashes from eddies at the foot of the noisy "shoals," and in the deeper, quieter stretches they came from the shadows of bottom "chunk rock." I could see their underwater gyrations through clear water from the drifting wooden johnboat.

I heard the loons on a Maine evening and I saw the bass appear from far down in the shadows of great granite boulders, small dark projectiles at first, shooting upward to take the bug hard. Maine was special for I had dreamed of it as a kid, reading of it from sporting magazines—things written by New York writers with pipes and old felt hats.

There is a special secret to bug fishing, which I shall now reveal. The secret is to visualize a bass—real or imaginary—who watches a bug's performance. Without this bass the routine casting and retrieving becomes pretty dull. All really good bug fishermen are aware of this fish although the subject is seldom mentioned.

When the bug arrives within his field of view this bass is either resting or feeding and his curiosity is aroused by the bug's presence. He moves over and lies somewhat below it and watches it carefully. When it begins to swim away slowly he may decide to grab it before it escapes. He may just swim along under it for more study. Now the bug pops and he may feel it is escaping and strikes hard. But if he is uncertain he continues to watch and the bug pops very loudly, throwing considerable water and obviously either making its getaway or showing fight.

Through a normal day's fishing a bug angler deals with hundreds of these real or imaginary fish and they sustain his enthusiasm, even though his waders leak and his elbow bothers him. Now and then there is someone who tries bug fishing and is not aware of the ghostly presence of such fish, so he usually quits bug casting and either confines his angling to trout or becomes a plastic worm expert. There are numerous corollaries to this situation. The golfer, for example, cannot always see the hole he is stalking.

After analysis, anyone can see there is not only technique but mysticism in bug fishing. It has been more difficult to bring bug construction into the hallowed status of tying trout flies. I'll admit a good bug maker can be awed by the production of a #22 dry fly. (For the edification of non-anglers, a #22 hook is smaller than you think it is, and once dropped on a carpet can be found only by bare feet.)

The bass bug suffers a little from lack of tradition and I can't find anything about it until around 1910 when Ernest H. Peckinpaugh of Chattanooga came up with some for bass fishing at night. In the twenties there were endless homemade variations, and after I began flailing in the thirties there were few completely new ideas. The Dalhberg Diver is a special form, a bug that dives when retrieved and becomes what my old friend Jack Gowdy called "wet bait." An artistic diving form was designed by the late Roy Berry of Kentucky about twenty years ago.

I am a little reticent about my own efforts in bug design. Needing a slow mover that would stay on the surface over eelgrass, I persuaded my wife to tie a long weedless streamer with an oval cork body fastened to the long hook shank. I called it the Slosher, I believe, although I once forgot that clever title and named it something else temporarily. A description appeared in a magazine (without illustration) and an ill-tempered reader wrote to the magazine that he saw where Waterman had "rediscovered the slider." The editor (may his advertisers forsake him) ran the reader's comment without giving me a chance to explain that my bug-streamer was completely different, the cork being behind some hackle instead of appearing as a head.

The bass bug fisherman has been treated a little like a poor relation by anglers fishing for what have become more glamorous species through long seniority and classic literature. There is, however, a subcurrent of bass anglers who make their own traditions, keeping them largely quiet.

While an Atlantic salmon angler and his guide approach a famous pool, the angler carefully checking his custom rod and his $600 reel, somewhere there is a bug fisherman on a shallow bass lake in a float tube (I first saw such a tube in the twenties) studying a patch of emergent arrowhead and a row of cattails. The sun is just down behind enormous thunderheads and there is insect hum along with the lazy calls of roost-bound crows.

The bug fisherman imagines the bass at the edge of the arrowhead and under the little patch of lily pads. He works out his line and he may have a $600 reel himself.

Chapter Six

THE PEASANT
TROUT

Famous trout streams are like old battlefields in that there seem to be unseen observers everywhere. On trout streams, I think they carry fine bamboo rods under their arms and wear old felt hats. Brown trout look much the same except for a little difference in color due to water and bottom. I don't think a Pennsylvania trout is any better than a Colorado trout or a North Carolina trout, but he's had better press. Letort trout are probably no better than those in obscure Pennsylvania creeks—they just live in a classy neighborhood and are watched. Before I threw a fly at the Letort I watched Harry Murray fish there. Since Harry Murray has been doing it for a long time, he is only slightly abashed by the Letort trout, and after he had caught three and left, I waded in carefully and looked around. I felt I was being watched but I saw no one at all.

I paid furtive attention to the shaded park benches that seemed a little strange to a fellow who began his fly fishing with green perch on Cow Creek in Kansas. The Letort water slid and curled and two good brown trout swam past, going upstream, just under the surface and about two feet apart. They'd told me there probably wouldn't be any insect hatch so I put on a cricket and worked a bank of vegetation, but nothing came of that. Then I saw the broad tail of a really big trout working something near the bottom against the underwater plants on the opposite shore. My cricket didn't go deep enough so I pawed my box nervously for some other things that Vince Marinaro, famous guardian of the stream, had recommended. Another pair of brown trout, about eighteen inches long, swam past, going upstream. A third pair came by and I wiped my glasses. Nothing I could throw to the trout with the waving tail got any results. I didn't even scare him and I wondered if Charlie Fox, beloved sage of the Letort, could have helped me. Another pair of eighteen-inch brown trout came past, headed upstream, not frightened, just traveling purposefully.

I had sighted another trout tipping up across the stream and was working line toward him when there was a splash at my right elbow, very close since I was in three feet of water. A moment later, it happened again, and this time I realized it was a fish striking something five feet from my waders. When it struck again, I saw it was a foot-long rainbow with a delinquent look about the eyes. And then I took my leader in my right hand, holding my rod with my left hand near the stripping guide so that it balanced, and I handlined the peasant trout so that he struck my imitation cricket wildly. After he was hooked I let him swing into the current and I played him carefully. As I released him I saw two more eighteen-inch browns go by, headed upstream. I waded ashore and stood on one of those rock walkways and surveyed the Letort with a calculating eye. After all, I had caught a fish there and could face the unseen trout-fishing spirits with confidence. Then I saw a real fisherman walking along well back from the stream and studying it carefully. I could see he was no stranger to the scene and I caught him studying me as well as the stream, possibly looking for a worm can or a stringer. "Hello!" I said.

"Could you tell me what those brown trout are doing when they go upstream in pairs like that?"

"I never saw them do that," he said. "Don't you think it was the same fish passing you more than once?" I never went into it any further. It was not the same fish; it was several pairs of fish, all about the same size, and the fact that not everyone knew about it or why it happened made me an authority—or almost an authority—on something about the Letort. A low sun formed shadows on the water. I could hear traffic on the great highways that Vince Marinaro had reported ruefully and I walked the bank slowly, looking for a rise and wondering about the big trout with their noses down. Then, in a twisted current by a little jam of a single log and a wad of tangled brush, a good trout rose twice. I worked out some line and dropped a fly there. I think it was a Light Cahill. He took it with a gulp, and as I played him carefully I felt I knew quite a bit about classic Pennsylvania water.

Chapter Seven

OUR
CREEK

Spring creeks with trout are hard to come by, even in the West where they are treasured by people with fine rods and boxes with very small flies that match or nearly match a great many hatched insects with long Latin names. They are often very public with waiting lists of those who will pay to fish them, and only rarely are they private places like ours.

We came to it by chance when we made friends with the owner, who was very seldom in that part of the country. He fenced away the cattle that had grazed its banks and cooled in its riffles, and he said maybe we could have the perfect trout stream. We were very near to that.

The stream itself was quite clear enough with shallow riffles that ran over rock and gravel, and there were places where water growth waved sinuously next to watercress. There were several sharp bends with deep-gouged and un-dercut banks, and when we first saw the creek there were gentle rises there, fish reaching for a tiny hatch we could not quite identify. We waded carefully and our casts had to be exact. The fish were not exceptionally selective if the fly was the right size and the cast perfect. There were rainbows, browns, and a few brook trout. Some of them were as much as fifteen inches long and twice we caught nineteen-inch fish, barely missing the magic twenty-inch mark.

By the second season we had established our wading approaches to the best spots and we had gone to two-weight rods for the 6X tippets and long leaders we needed. By then we knew about where to stand for the best casts and we knew a dozen spots where good fish generally were. We learned to approach the creek carefully, for with the cattle gone *our* fish were sensitive to heavy feet as much as ten yards from the shoreline, even at the bend with the high bank. It was the third year when my wife Debie caught the nineteen-incher on a tiny caddis fly, steering her fish breathlessly past a bank of watercress that seemed to grow toward the boils her brown trout was making.

That was the year I could see the big rainbow rising at the fence at the end of *our* property, and put a scraggly Light Cahill in exactly the right place, only to tighten up too much when he lunged under the wire. I have lost larger fish but I can still see his gaudy flank catching the afternoon sun. And there was the really good brown that made a great vee from near the shoreline to take a shaggy little emerger I was working over a pod of lesser midstream diners. The fishing was difficult, dainty, and wonderful, but there were other things.

Our creek is in a great valley with mountains on two sides, sometimes holding a little snow in early summer. In evening there would often be a ragged line of arguing Canada geese, and *every* evening there would be a flock of sandhill cranes going to their roost near the creek, coming in with their musical ratchet calls and in silhouette appearing to be from another world.

There were pheasants in a patch of brush in one bend and white-tailed deer left bedding outlines. In late summer there were mallard and teal nests, the hens ruining fishing for two hundred yards with their squawking and floundering as they feigned life-threatening injuries.

There were the eerie winnowing sounds of Wilson snipe overhead at their mating time—sounds I did not recognize at first although I had hunted them for many years a thousand miles south of the creek. And when I looked up at the hovering clowns I saw a backdrop of airliner contrails in an unbelievably deep blue sky.

I am not sure just how many years we had *our* creek, opening the combination lock each day with the self-importance of the privileged few shutting out the world. But suddenly one summer there were only fingerlings in the bends and no gliding flotillas of freshly hatched flies.

"Your creek has silted in," the fisheries biologist said. "The only thing you can do is install a sediment trap."

I suppose this must be done but how can a contraption like that save an entire private world like *our* creek?

Chapter Eight

SPRING

CREEKS

They told me long ago that to start an article on fishing you need a paragraph of action involving a large fish. In keeping with this formula I shall begin with my wife running at top speed downstream in eighteen inches of water.

Some distance ahead of my wife was a rapidly moving vee in the center of a glistening meadow stream and her rod was bent toward it. Even small wives running downstream make considerable noise in eighteen inches of water, but as mine went around a bend her comments were easily audible. It seems someone had not put backing on the reel that went with her four-weight fly rod (I never expected big fish with that little rig) and the moral, it seems, was that if you want a thing done well you should do it yourself. As I contemplated Debie's receding wake, I recalled that I had agreed to put a new line on her reel if she would tie me two #20 no-hackle emerger flies.

My wife's four-pound rainbow trout, running and jumping against a 6X tippet testing around two pounds, is a mite unusual on a western spring creek, but it is good to get it in here since there is a persistent rumor that only tiddlers live in such waters. There are a few deep-wading, double-hauling types who scorn flies that are hard to see on dull days, and most spring creeks are best fished with little things. My wife frequently casts what she calls "teeny-weenies," and I at first thought that category covered all very small flies but I have learned since that "hangy-downies," for example, are equally small but completely different. My wife has simplified the nomenclature of dry flies and small nymphs to the point that only she and a few of her friends know what she is talking about. I am on the edge of that circle, sometimes wishing she would use the Latin names and conventional pattern designations, for I could at least look those up somewhere.

I am also afraid that Debie will embarrass me by exposing her ignorance of conventional fly patterns in the company of technical anglers. However, I find that while Debie does not revert to Latin and traditional pattern names in the company of those who have written books on the subject, the experts have a tendency to degenerate into her primitive vocabulary and are likely to speak freely of *teeny-weenies* and *hangy-downies* while in her company.

This is about spring creeks rather than about Debie, but since she is a "spring-creek fisherman," and since we have this close association, it is impossible to leave her out completely. I believe her informal approach is rather unusual among spring-creek fisherpersons, but evidently it does not bar her from the cult. I am quite aware that there are veteran spring-creek followers who spend long winter evenings producing delicately beautiful little flies with exotic fur and feathers from the ends of the earth. Debie, however, is apt to pile her waders and rod case on the floor a few minutes before time to leave and then rummage through a rather grimy vest to "see what I need." She then sits down at a tying vise, paws through some piles of odds and ends, and produces strange little things that catch a great many fish. Time is short, she explains, because she had to have her nails done and patch her waders. Sounds pretty sloppy, and I guess it is. But evidently she buys the best in basic fly materials, insisting on top-notch hackle, even though she may tie almost anything in with it. Because there aren't many women spring-creek addicts, Debie may get a higher rating than she deserves.

They call them "spring creeks" in the West. In the East they have called them "limestone creeks," and in Britain, where all of our fancy fly fishing got its start, they call them "chalk streams." This, of course, is a pretty juvenile description for a student of the matter, but it is surprising how many trout anglers don't know why a spring creek is different from what we call a "freestone stream."

A true spring creek is fed almost entirely from springs, getting only a little runoff from rain or snow, and it's pretty alkaline, which means a lot of underwater vegetation, for one thing. The word is "lush." Underwater vegetation is great for insect life, and a trout living in spring creek water will continue to feed on insects after a fish of the same size in other waters would be looking for something with meat on its bones. A haughty mayfly-matching spring-creek angler might call that cannibalism.

So, while an eighteen-inch brown or rainbow trout in most rivers would be stalking various sorts of minnows, a spring-creek resident would be waiting for a batch of mayflies and might be sipping them with a delicacy that causes the faithful to quiver uncontrollably over their split-bamboo rods. Actually, your true spring-creeker is more likely to call his a "cane" rod. It would sound better if graphite hadn't been so successful in the rod-making business, and bamboos are getting scarce. Anyway, Debie has a Leonard for calm days and a Jenkins for the wind.

Anyone who has sought wild and scenic rivers through the years is likely to be a little taken aback by stiles over fences and "fishing huts." At the Letort in Pennsylvania there are those carefully positioned steps to stand on while you cast and sort your flies, or lick your wounds on well-built benches.

The West came around rather slowly to the formal trout-stream concept. First, the buffalo got scarce, then they strung barbed wire all over the country, and a few years back I stared speechless at a shelter with a picnic table inside for the use of anglers on Armstrong Spring Creek near Livingston, Montana. Not far away is equally famous Nelson's Spring Creek with picnic tables and outdoor toilet (other spring creeks have the latter too). There are many streams, even those without paid fishing, that now are enclosed by cow- and sheep-proof fences.

I can recall when an inquiry as to the cost of a "rod" on a western spring creek met with considerable merriment, but now it's a common term for a period of paid fishing. For a long time the natives considered toll fishing a sort of tourist entrapment, but they know now that it's what saved some of the finest trout water in the world—and the natives now make their reservations the same as out-of-staters. These aren't tenderfoot catch-out ponds.

For years, many eastern anglers who went West were interested mainly in big fish that were caught by standing up to your shirt pockets in the biggest rivers and throwing all of the feathers a chicken could spare. Those were bigger fish than they'd had back East or even in the northern Midwest. The insects out West were different and followed different rules. The mammoth stoneflies that hatched on many western rivers in midsummer were nearly enough matched by scary and hairy things that even a beginner could tie with a little thread and odds and ends of fuzz and feathers.

But all this time there were a few characters with light rods and tiny flies who had found a sort of super edition of what they'd had back home. They were into the spring creeks with very little splashing.

Then when trout fishermen learned more Latin and more and more of them became uppity with "cane" rods and nothing but English reels and enormous aluminum fly boxes, the western spring creeks began to come into their own and needed protection. A good spring creek was too fragile for unlimited public access and the land it ran through became

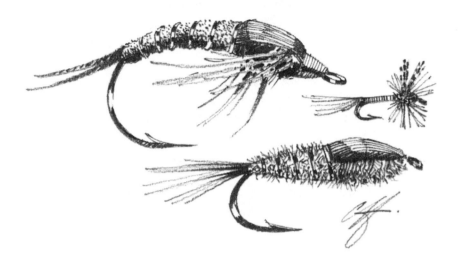

expensive. At first the local folks snarled at the idea of paid fishing, but when a few choice spring creeks were leased or bought outright, leaving the public with their noses pressed against "No Trespassing" signs, it was no longer disgraceful to help a rancher with his taxes. "Wild and scenic" rivers were fine, but available meadow streams were getting scarce.

A western spring creek is probably on private property, simply because valleys with reliable streams looked pretty good to early homesteaders—and today it appears that good trout water is more valuable by the acre than pasture, alfalfa, or grain. Where Debie chased the big rainbow around the bend there were a lot more big fish and we finished the day in a sort of daze, muttering incoherently about six-pound trout that took #20 dry flies in dainty, sipping rises. Standing in eighteen inches of water and planning an approach to an arrogant monster a hundred feet away, I contemplated the fact that such a stream could be ruined in a few days of public fishing. Clear, shallow water and very big fish. No matter how carefully we waded there was little use in working a pool more than once in four or five hours—and it was impossible to catch much from the banks since from those shallow runs we stood out like what we were—strange-shaped predators with fiend-ish weapons.

We'd gotten on that water by a devious route, and by acci-dent since we hadn't known about it and had simply accepted a fishing invitation. I learned the place was for sale and that a tentative deal was actually in the works. I did not consider bidding for this particular trout heaven since the discussed price was something over four million dollars and I was a little pinched because our house needed painting.

We first started fishing the western spring creeks a long time ago, and although we don't cast any better than we did then and haven't learned much more about trout biology, we have acquired some low cunning that helps us from time to time. For example, faithful matching of spring-creek hatches is no longer at the top of our list. The other day I went to buy some #20 Tricos and told the man we were doing very well on Nelson's Spring Creek. He said there is no Trico hatch at Nelson's but Debie and I (she cannot pronounce *tricorythodes* any better than I can) had been on a roll with them. Debie said to buy them as she was not good on tying Tricos.

We have learned that in those very small flies trout some-times choose something they never saw before. There was a time when there was a 10 A.M. to 2 P.M. hatch on Armstrong Spring Creek, matched pretty well by a #16 Light Cahill. In fact, the late Dan Bailey once said his only complaint with the stream was that the fly selection was pre-ordained and the fishing was from ten to two. For better or worse, there have been many changes on Armstrong's (including an overpower-ing flood) and the fish are no longer so consistent. I am sure many of the faithful like it better the way it is now. At one time there was often no one at all on the creek in late after-noon. They just didn't bother.

Debie began making a daily trip to Armstrong's, getting there in late afternoon and doing much of her fishing well upstream, just above and below the "big" spring that rattles down over the rocks from near a barn and ranch house. For several years she had that almost entirely to herself, and when

I would go along and fail to understand the nuances of her approach she would try to be nice although quivering with frustration. She was and is very strong on "emergers," those creatures in the act of changing from nymphs to flies, and specialized in fishing in the surface film.

Most of us discover, from time to time, a slightly different approach at one of the spring creeks, make a killing of a day or two and smugly confide our secret only to our closest friends or our bankers. There was the man who caught twenty-five or thirty trout on an ant pattern, fishing it along the shoreline, and announced that spring creeks no longer had any mystery for him. On his next trip he caught no fish at all on the ant. Sometimes an ant against the shoreline is good for me and sometimes I might as well be casting an overshoe. I once tore things up with a beetle tied by Harry Murray of Virginia (a noted innovator) and thought that was the true answer, but on another trip the trout eyed it as they would a grenade. As elsewhere, the nymph fishermen are most deadly of all on most of the spring creeks and some of the best are short-line operators who stand like herons in the midst of rising trout.

The commercialized creeks probably have more fish per acre than any others. They're generally flies-only and catch-and-release-only and, as this is written, fifty dollars a day is a fairly standard rod fee—but trout are victims of inflation too. There's a quota of fishermen per day, generally religiously adhered to. Many who are short on spring creek experience hire guides, most of whom are true experts. After all, you can't conscientiously charge a man a guide fee for simply showing him where the creek is. Someone having limited time certainly starts much faster with a guide, even if he's an expert somewhere else.

Broad pods of big trout rising steadily in two feet of clear water over swaying underwater fields of green vegetation are heady stuff, especially with a background of tall cottonwoods, ranch buildings, and the Rocky Mountains. They're wild trout, all right, but on the commercialized streams they see fishermen every day and the newcomer sometimes does not understand that while they accept him as mobile scenery they have examined his flies and his waders and have no intention of striking for him. So he stands too long without moving his feet very much, thinking that as long as the fish are rising within an easy cast there must be some way of catching them. He'll probably do better to move a little and try some new targets. There are somewhat different problems, though, on creeks where there is a very slight pressure and a single sloppy cast will draw an evacuation instead of a fishy yawn.

There are some divisions in the spring-creek ranks. Some nymph fishermen may tell you in private that their delicate feel for underwater-takes leads to greatest satisfaction, and there are others who feel the real game is to bring a trout to the surface. For the surface operator, the crowning reward is to see a fish take an artificial with the same move it has been using for natural flies—and an extra splash or too fast a turn shows that the take was not completely successful, even if the fish is caught. (I have heard of landscape painters who felt it was not ethical to use photographs in aiding their impressions.)

The western spring creeks are regular pilgrimages for many anglers from all over the world, but there are westerners who go to wade in Catskill waters, not for better fishing but to feel the tradition and commune with ghosts of anglers past. Most of the technical western anglers specialize in a single stream, but a regular follower of Depuy's Creek in Montana is likely to have waded Idaho's Silver Creek at some time.

We grin at those who plot for months or years and travel thousands of miles, approaching a murmuring little stream as if it were some sort of baptismal font. I explain this in telling of the time I fumbled awkwardly in a spring creek full of rising trout, finally catching a single juvenile brown after tangling in a bush and breaking a tippet. I heard polite hand-clapping and looked up to see a little group of watchers in street clothes.

They had come hundreds of miles to see that spring creek. They were not good enough to actually fish it, they said, and after they left I probably looked as stupid as I felt.

Chapter Nine

HIGHER TROUT

These creeks and their trout attracted early settlers and, before them, mountain men with beaver traps and the ruffed grouse and deer that lived there with the beaver. Beaver trappers came 170 years ago not knowing where they were and not caring. All they needed to remember was the way out—which was simply downstream to the flats and to the river and to rendezvous. If they never came out they stayed in unmarked graves. Or no graves at all.

Where the beaver trappers worked or wintered is conjecture and it may be that my creek had none of them at all. But I defy you to prove they were not there, for the beaver are, and downstream where the canyon becomes a valley the soil is largely a product of silted ponds of long ago—thousands of years.

The wild trout of the backcountry know no Latin and their defense is not a careful selection of catalogued nymphs and emerging caddis or mayflies but a watchfulness for strange things that move, hover, or splash. In the little high-country creeks a kingfisher's shadow remains important to fish that have only recently outgrown the bird's appetite. Backcountry trout must be stalked for they are vulnerable from nearby banks, living in a small world, and their prey is judged mainly by size. Delicate subtlety of fly pattern is seldom a problem.

There are specialists in backwoods trout fishing. My old friend Jack Ward was surprised that I didn't know his basic operating procedure for the really tiny creeks. Always had done it, he said. You just wade in above the pool you like and stir up a little mud. You cast your fly, wet or dry, downstream as the mud arrives at the chosen spot. I wanted to know why it works, thinking it involved a breakthrough in trout psychology, but Jack had no answer and seemed to think I was complicating an essentially simple operation. I do not want to complicate it further but the drifting mud means rain or disturbance, either of which may dislodge food.

The creek that slides and rattles past the old homestead is just a little big for the mud trick. In its riffles it is only a few inches deep but the outsides of its sharp bend areas are undercut, the water going under stones or roots, and when you slosh into such a place to recover your snagged fly you're surprised to find the water is almost to the top of your hip boots.

The dry fly is easiest. In midsummer it can imitate a grasshopper, but patterns are seldom important. You come up from below and study the possibilities for a backcast. Your rod is light but it isn't a treasure because the backcountry is hard on tackle.

Find the place to cast from, probably a sandy bar with deer tracks, and throw the fly where the little ridge of fast water begins to spread below midpool. The water is clear but you don't see the fish lying near the stony bottom until he has darted into position and then slowed to take the fly from below. It's good if it's a cutthroat, a "native," for that better fits the setting, but it could be a brook trout, rainbow, or brown trout, long removed from their hatchery ancestors.

If I am doing the fishing, I plot against what should be the largest fish in the pool. The deep, undercut area is harder to reach and I change position a little. The fly must land above it, and there are likely to be sweeping branches or projecting roots as it comes down to swing almost out of sight.

First, a tentative cast a little too far out, just to see if everything is working, and another that almost but not quite swings over the target area. Then I lengthen the line a few inches and make my try, which may result in the fly catching ignominiously in a branch, root, or grassy sweeper. But if nothing goes wrong it will float bouncily back within inches of the darkly shadowed undercut and I may see an indistinct gleam of color beneath it, distorted by a dozen miniature currents, before the fly is taken or refused. A refusal will probably result from some treacherous slab of current that tugs at the leader and causes the fly to make a distinct wake, exaggerating drag that sends the trace of submerged color back into darkness.

At that point I get a false sense of being a part of the scene, understanding trout and backcountry creeks, and I plan an elaborate curlicue of fancy casting which I am sure will present a new fly perfectly to the fish that showed a broad side for a magnified second. Concentration. And that is when I feel my backcast catch a tall willow or a groping pine. Reality. The fly is probably too high to reach.

Such things are scorned by those who feel success or failure may depend upon selection of a female mayfly imitation instead of a male. My tactics are backwoods crudity when observed by learned anglers casting for fish that are themselves students of entomology and wader trademarks.

There are beaver pond specialists like the late Dan Bailey.

He admitted the limestone spring creeks were more challenging in their way, but said the beaver ponds were more lonely places—and surprising, each different, for a successful beaver dam can separate two little trout worlds. It can divide them by both size and species, and a casual fisherman who leaves one because it is crowded with stunted brook trout may walk past a big Loch Leven living in the one below it, sulking among lesser fish.

Above the old homestead, where the canyon opens up again, generations of beavers have changed the landscape by design and accident, their structural failures contributing almost as much as their successes. Where a super-dam has held there is a lake like a miniature of some TVA impoundment, the old stream bed making a deep, meandering groove far out on its bottom, a place where really good trout live.

Where some over-enthusiastic toothy construction team has bungled a pretentious edifice, spring floods have broken through, the separated main timbers jutting forlornly into a little torrent of falling water. But a fisherman studies the place carefully because the waterfall has gouged out a hole at its base, a deep new pool. Put the big hair-winged fly near where the bubbles come up from the deepest part.

Mallard hens nest at the beaver ponds, quacking loudly to scare fish and fisherman when he cautiously pokes his head above a big dam to aim a cast where he thinks the old streambed probably went.

Old homesteads and the creeks that attracted them draw few fishermen. Below them are the rivers with bigger trout and the technical streams attended by learned anglers with deep fly boxes and entomological texts. Above them are the high-country creeks that draw the hikers with cleated leather boots instead of waders and the midsummer horse-packing parties who camp by icy trickles where hard-bodied little fish flash at skimpy food.

Perhaps half a mile is the magic distance. Half a mile above the larger streams the anglers with the big fly boxes and fine rods tend to turn back toward bigger water. And no muscular young hiker with a pack rod, freeze-dried provisions, and a mountain tent will stop at half a mile. So perhaps the old homesteads with the overgrown roads are visited least of all.

But the season is short. Even summer is cool in the canyon and when September anglers at lower altitude begin to splice heavier leaders for "fall fishing" and the hikers give way to big-game hunters with grinding gears or creaking saddles, the fishing falls off in my canyon as it does in many others.

The old log house seems to have settled even more, its outlines softened by snow, and there are no beaver trappers wintering in the meadows. The trout are under ice in deep holes.

Chapter Ten

SUNKEN TREASURE

Listory, mystery, and millions of fish linger around wrecks; it is almost a shame that modern divers can reach them. I become serious when I see the charts showing wrecks that dot the Atlantic off Cape Hatteras, and the bottomed fleets of World War II that will be seen for lifetimes in the South Pacific shallows. When a knowing captain positioned us over a wreck off Hatteras, he moved several times before he was in exactly the right place and nodded with satisfaction when he saw a little blob of oil that rose from the ship below—oil that had been leaking for generations.

Wrecks are monuments to great wars and great storms, and if there are really such things as ghosts they must certainly live among sunken ships. For some, this may make wreck fishing somewhat sacrilegious, but for most of us a wreck fish just brings a little something special with it.

The first wreck fishing I did was over some sort of sunken commercial craft that was barely covered at low tide, and it was located just off some small islands on Florida's lower west coast. I went there with an old-timer who had regularly located it by what appeared to be some kind of mangrove magic, and his triangulation was accomplished by simply slowing down and glancing in two or three directions.

But that morning there was no need for special navigation, for someone had beaten us there. Barely visible in a dense fog and dead calm was a figure with a long pole and a weathered skiff. He used live bait and seemed to be almost constantly heaving on some splashing giant. When he was not fighting a fish we could see a crisp outline of the wreck in eerie detail, inscribed in small baitfish at the surface, even to its engine parts. Now and then the bait would scatter from an attack and then would regroup almost instantly in its original design. The indistinct figure in the old skiff had the best spot, but we managed to slip out an anchor and throw streamer flies at the wreck's outline.

We were not as efficient as our competitor, but we had strikes from big snook, red drum, and a crashing tarpon that disrupted things for a while. Eventually the fog lifted, the sun came out, the tide began to fill, and a little breeze rippled the surface where the baitfish had been. Nothing more followed our lures.

For thirty years we fished for bonefish near a small wreck on a Florida Keys reef. The wooden structure vanished before long and the last time I was there nothing much was left except the engine and some other metal parts sinking into the bottom, barnacle-encrusted and invisible at high tide. It had been my marker for all that time and often there was an evil-eyed barracuda on it, making largely futile passes at baitfish that scooted into crannies.

I once wheeled an outboard through the Everglades' creeks and bays and slipped up to an abandoned cabin boat that sat on the bottom with its bow resting on a little mangrove island. I told my guest to cast just ahead of the steering wheel and he lost his plug on something large and noisy. Last year I went back to the island but the old cruiser had disappeared after twenty years. Wrecks, like fishermen, don't last forever.

Section Two

WINGSHOOTING

Chapter Eleven

REPORTS FROM THE FIELD

Even a Christmas card can start it. Anyone who has climbed hills and waded marshes with shotguns for a long time remembers special times and places, some of which he will not feel or see again. With time the memories become more valued, and if they are dimmed it is always for the better, the patina of years smoothing the rough spots and accenting the joys.

I lack the sophistication of a world traveler, still marveling at quick transportation and even today's swift telephone connections. It is incredible to me that I can stand in a Colombia valley and watch the doves sweep down from the Andes when yesterday I was checking my gun at a Miami airport desk. And I am appalled that there is a shopping mall where I once found bobwhite quail in the pines.

Stay at it long enough and anyone who labors over outdoor scribbling will find he has unknown readers around the country who have followed him through the years, no matter if he is no household word, and they send him letters from places he has been and written about.

In August there is a note from Alaska, and although it makes no mention of ptarmigan I know the beginnings of Alaska's early fall when the caribou are becoming a little restless. Years ago there was heavy fog north of Fairbanks where the dog pointed ptarmigan that matched the blotchy rocks scattered on the tundra. It rained on us and bush planes passed below our little mountain, following a highway. The sound of my shots seemed to die in the fog. We ate ptarmigan daily and swore it was better than pheasant. We compared it to ruffed grouse but swore never to do so in the company of dedicated ruff hunters. My new over-under rusted on the way home, stored against the uninsulated camper wall.

There is a letter from a hunter in Oregon, who has the gall to make the notation *Chukar Country* after his address. For an overage chukar chaser *that* is an unkind cut. In Oregon that first time I followed a dog along a bluff high over the Malheur River and looked far down where a row of pheasant hunters walked across a field and their shots came to me long after I saw the tiny puffs of smokeless powder smoke from their guns.

Up there the chukars were bunched in coveys among the rocks, and several times I saw their sentries atop boulders. The dog pointed and I shot chukars and never saw another chukar hunter, although the pheasant finders could be heard all day as faint pops. It is the edge of desert country, and I have been back since to climb the sides of great erosions and listen to the gentle cackles of one of the world's greatest game birds. I remember the flocks of partridge sailing over the river far below, tilting with changing air currents and disappearing somewhere in brush and stone. It was near there that a hunting golden eagle found a covey for me, stopping his tireless gliding to descend abruptly over birds that found shelter in time. And then they escaped me, too, diving steeply while I tried to point a gun muzzle at a fleeting glimpse between the boulders.

The note from Alberta takes me to a year of drought when we used binoculars from a promontory at dawn and a fine goose hunter somehow figured where the great flocks were feeding each morning—watching the wavering lines of birds over a hundred square miles of dry prairie, soon to be distorted by heat mirage. And when we dug the pits it was hardpan that demanded picks as well as shovels, but the geese came unafraid to the set, more geese than anyone needed. The man who planned the shoot was a master. Still, I remember best the distant undulating lines of birds seen through binoculars over the dry prairie as the sun came up red.

I heard from the man who owned the ranch where I shot the gobbler. He no longer owns it and lives nowhere near it, but there was the collection of gobbler's beards posted in the big room that somehow stated it had been there for a long time and would be there for a long time to come. I am not much of a turkey hunter and I sat in heavy predawn rain, following the instructions of a master guide. The instructions were mainly to be silent and motionless while the rain came down, and when I shot the gobbler and it disappeared from view behind the fringe of grass and weeds, the straight-down rain seemed to drum harder. The beard from my gobbler was not as long as most of the others that had been saved for the big room, but my host put mine up all those years ago and I wonder if it is still there.

There's a card from British Columbia that doesn't mention grouse, but more than twenty years ago some cutover there was in just the right stage of succession, and when the season opened there were coveys of young ruffs that flushed reluctantly before a pop-eyed dog, and there were crusty adults that disputed the way on some of the riverside trails, walking off with great dignity and reluctant to fly—but when they flew they went as grouse are supposed to go, swinging through the willows and pines. Being a greenhorn at the grouse business, I did not realize I was viewing something few gunners will ever see. They called them "willow grouse."

There have been other times when I have been on the scene at the peak of a population cycle, but there were also years when I went at the wrong times and the birds were "down." Strangely, I recall them just as well, remembering the few birds I shot a little guiltily—as I did in South Dakota when the prairie chickens were scarce. There was heat and drought that time, and when I finally found some birds, and had killed two of a covey, I watched my dog point two singles and then saw them fly away. I swung the gun up but didn't shoot and smiled when I put it down. Those chickens were having hard time enough without my interference. And this year I heard from Pierre that drought and heat have put the birds down again, bringing back the memories of crunchy dry grass and noisy throngs of grasshoppers. In between, there have been better years in South Dakota.

My old friend, the Texas quail hunter, says on the phone that it is a good year there. When I first hunted Texas quail I did it in the border brush country of cactus and thorns. That is not the most easy quail habitat in the state, but I had wanted to walk through it since childhood and at every arroyo imagined a nineteenth-century cowboy chousing a lean, mean-eyed longhorn. What really had sent me down there was a painting of two modern quail shooters with two modern pointers in the cactus. I did not kill many birds on that trip but I felt superior to those who had shot Texas quail more comfortably.

The man sent us a Christmas greeting from Tennessee, where he lives, but it was in Alabama that I hunted bobwhite quail with him. I doubt if he remembers the same things about the trip that I do. You see, he is one of those master specialists, and quail and quail dogs had been a part of his life for so long that his seemingly occult knowledge of the birds was routine to him. I am older than he is, but I was so transfixed by his operation that I fumbled as if I had never hunted any kind of birds before.

I saw a covey go up wild where he couldn't watch it and I detailed to him where it had headed and must have landed. But when we got there with a dog he seemed to be thinking of something else, and when we had covered the area I had chosen I was a little embarrassed for there were no birds there at all. Then he turned, apparently at random, and the dog began finding scattered singles.

"They hooked off this way," said the man from Tennessee, as if it was pure coincidence, too polite to say he had known it all along.

Then there was the bunch that scattered in skimpy cover, and while we walked through it he shot bird after bird. I did not get a shot. He apologized that it was easy to tell where the birds would be holding where he had walked. Oh, sure. If the man from Tennessee reads this—I am no hotshot but I am a hell of a lot better gunner than you probably think. You had me dazzled.

When I am in Florida it is sometimes nice to hear from the North. The freeways here are backed up and big, grumbling powerboats stir the rivers where I used to hear the wood ducks squeal as they came over the treetops. They fanned their rudder tails when they saw me and my gun. The weather map makes me a little pensive. I can see that arctic chill sweeping down from Alaska and into Montana and I know the ducks will really move before it.

"We're gonna get it now," says the cheerful telephone voice. "It's beginning to snow and blow up here."

Word from up there sharpens my recall. I can remember the days when I stumbled to the spring creek as most other water froze. I would carry a few decoys, and I wore enough clothing that I must have looked like a rag bag with feet. It would be a late dawn and the warm creek water built a towering wall of steam above it where the leafless cottonwoods cracked with ice. The mallards would come to the creek, small contingents breaking away from big flocks just arrived from Canada.

"Those aren't local ducks," we'd tell each other as we tried to get into shooting position in our makeshift blind. "Those are *northerns*!"

A northern mallard might be little different from resident ducks but it brought glamour and winter with it. I wonder if my friendly telephone caller realized he had encouraged my dreaming. For the moment the southland seemed dull.

I no longer get letters from northern California and I'm afraid all those folks from there are gone, for it has been a long while. Families don't have time to run down all of the faraway folks a man got acquainted with when he read about the outdoors, and when he's gone his letters just stop.

Somewhere up there I sat in a muddy ditch behind a bunch of goose decoys and watched the low flight of specklebellies coming to us, noisy in the early morning calm. Of course I shot too soon and the old goose hunter told me they were bigger than ducks. I can't even remember the name of the nearest town but I can see the geese coming in a leisurely and sinuous line and I wonder what is being done with that land today.

"There are more doves than ever," the old friend wrote. "Bunch of us are going down to Argentina and if you want to come along I'll promise you more shooting than you've ever had."

I haven't been to Argentina for a long time, but I can't get going so quick any more and I can't shoot the way that bunch does.

Chapter Twelve

BETTER THAN AVERAGE SHOTGUNS

It has always disturbed me that for all practical purposes a rusty pumpgun built in 1900 can kill upland birds and ducks as well as a gold inlaid double produced by an artist last year. If dead birds were the only objective, a great deal of expense and effort could have been spared.

But there is a complex status situation here. I knew a prosperous gunner who deliberately rusted his engraved Parker so it wouldn't look new. I chased birds with a fine shot who used a very old Model 12 Winchester pump with a solid rib and, savoring its dull-silver patina, would have fought to the death anyone who suggested renewing the bluing. I knew an expert quail shooter who carried a riot gun in the Dixie palmettos, although he had some pretty guns at home. He kept snickering about it, which made me uncomfortable.

There is the "classic bird gun," admired by almost a hundred years of shooters, and I can describe it without a dissenting vote, I am sure. I think we had better get it out of the way first.

The classic bird gun is a side-by-side double. It either has no pistol grip at all or has a semi-pistol grip, which has little or no effect on its feel or use, and it has a "splinter" fore-end. It is quite light, weighing substantially less than seven pounds in 12-gauge, and as chosen by Americans it usually has rather short barrels, longer in Europe. I guess it got its start in England, where people have shot well for a long time, and where sportsmen have been just a mite hard-headed about proper defense against driven grouse and pheasants.

The splinter fore-end (sounds like an American term) is a little checkered sliver of wood that encourages a rather short hold on the barrels. The British keep explaining that it is for holding the gun together rather than for grabbing in the heat of battle. They advocate reaching much farther out along the barrel, and you can buy those leather handguards to keep your hand from getting hot out there. This bothers me no end, for the colonists, who generally advise a shorter hand hold, have regularly used a longer fore-end.

Just when I thought sexism was pretty well stamped out in the upland covers, a lady had a long fore-end built for her high-grade double so she could follow the British instruction of a long reach without fear of her gun rusting inside the leather handguard. I think she is accepted at all only because she is very pretty and wears beautifully tailored shooting clothes.

I qualify as an authority on all of this stuff because I have an English shotgun. I got a leather handguard but it was the wrong size and every time I fired it would slide my hand way out toward the muzzle with the recoil. I gave it away, and so did the fellow I presented it to. He denies his ingratitude but I could swear I saw another acquaintance using it on a 10-gauge goose gun. It was supposed to be for 12-gauge.

It is hard to argue against the 12-gauge, with its endless load combinations, as a practical game gatherer. The 20 can be made lighter and almost as potent, although it has a harder time with its patterns in the heaviest loads. The 28 is a pres-

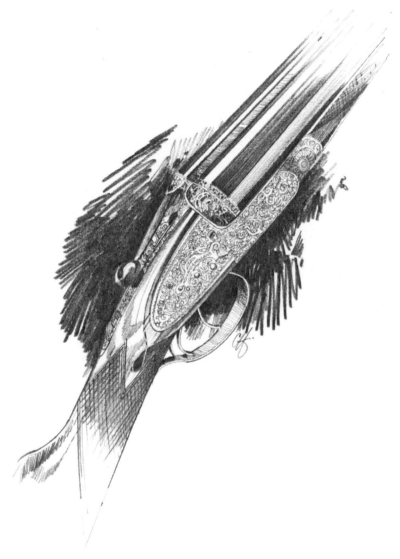

tige passion and uses a beautifully balanced shell, although a mite light for things like pheasants or western prairie birds. The 16-gauge, a favorite in Europe, has been called the perfect upland gauge, but was ostracized when left out of the American skeet programs years ago. Its popularity has been geographic and there have been quite a number of 16s in the South all along. This caused department store buyers to make some northern mistakes. I once found some northwestern stores trying so hard to get rid of overstocked 16-gauge shells that it was worthwhile to buy a 16, just to get a lifetime of inexpensive ammunition.

The little .410, drooled over by collectors, can be used by careful experts for things like quail and woodcock. Most of us should keep it as a pet, but some fine ones are put to strange uses. An owner bragged that his $30,000 side-by-side .410 is excellent at potting grouse off branches for big-game camp meat. A Lamborghini would be nice for newspaper delivery if it had more storage space.

I guess the most remarkable things about upland guns in the past forty years are the boom in over-unders and the production of precisely made choke tubes. A few years back you'd have had to install a choke device in a Holland & Holland over the owner's body, but I understand quite a few "best" grade guns are getting them added these days. In a way, they cut into sales because a fistful of easily installed choke tubes can take the place of separate barrels and more guns. Many people who buy really expensive guns, however, are not going to be deterred by practicality.

Although autoloaders and pumpguns are treated like land mines by the upper crust of game shooting, the over-under causes game-gun experts to take photos and draw diagrams to illustrate supremacy of the classic side-by-side without such gadgetry as ventilated ribs and single triggers. They would rather not be told that competitive shooters nearly all choose a single sighting plane.

The over-under's popularity in America has been explained by the fact we are "a nation of riflemen and repeating shotguns" and are thus wedded to the single sighting plane. But after smoldering for many years, the sporting clays game got really hot in Britain, mainland Europe, and the United States, and when competition really turned upward, the hardware winners tended toward over-unders and some autoloaders.

Through all of this learned survey, note we're dealing with gun lovers willing to spend plenty for pretty ones. There are dog experts, woodsmen, and game-bird authorities who consider guns as just essential tools and don't even notice a little rust—or crude stocks that look like discarded berry crate wood.

Shooters who feel they are ready to graduate from ordinary shotguns and want something special can sometimes face the same type of problems met by the happy soul who feels he is ready to shift from the family sedan to an exotic sports car. In many cases a 1980 Chevrolet is more reliable than a hundred thousand dollars worth of touchy adjustments. The local gunsmith isn't likely to have an ejector part for an Italian masterpiece exhibiting Pan and a chorus of prancing maidens on the sideplates. This was emphasized by the man who was showing me a finely engraved 28.

"It's never been fired," he said, "and maybe it's not supposed to be."

I went quail hunting with a real wizard who can afford fine guns and was carrying a new one. His dog pointed.

"If I fire this damned thing it will cost me $2,000 in depreciation," he said.

He killed a bird but didn't seem very enthusiastic for a few minutes.

Now engraving and inlays don't contribute much to shooting efficiency but can be pretty important. There are lovers of great detail in engraving and others who don't want it at all. There are, of course, many schools of engraving, the images going all the way from delicate scrolls to the over-under I noted with a beautifully done image (in gold) of a bull being belted on the stern with a bass fiddle. There have been Elvis Presley in action and Washington crossing the Delaware. Some of the owners are proud of how much they spent and others are secretive.

Americans are more choosy about wood, I think, than shooters from England and Europe. I have seen some beautiful European guns with stocks apparently constructed from sawmill scrap, and one had a patched knothole that showed when the finish began to wear. Choice figured-stock-wood comes from old trees that have been thirsty all their lives and produce tortured grain. One custom gunsmith told me the general public was most impressed by a carved and dyed stock in his window, whittled during slow periods by "a kid who works down at the hamburger place." No one mentioned the classic checkering designs next to it.

Far from home, repairs become mighty important. In a fit of conscientious research I cornered a well-known gunsmith, who has built guns from scratch, and asked him what gun he would choose if he were going into a wilderness with no access to tools he couldn't carry in his pockets. He didn't hesitate and announced it would be a Remington Model 870 pumpgun. (Dear Remington: Send my new 870, care of the publisher.)

"Bird gun" covers a broad territory and I am intrigued by those chosen by dove shooters in Central and South America, where some experts fire two thousand shots a day. They lean toward gas-operated semi-autos (minimum recoil) and carry little boxes of carefully chosen and inexpensive repair parts. In some localities they are allowed to bring in only one gun but additional barrels are okay.

American shooters have been lovers of large noises and hard kicks ever since ammunition makers started giving their shells names that sound like the crack of doom. When the occasional hunter misses badly he naturally assumes he needs more powder and shot, a contention scorned by owners of fine game guns, which like to come apart with heavy loads. The English tend toward short shells with light charges, and new owners of British guns have taken a superior attitude in explaining to me that light loads and open bores are enough for anything I'm likely to encounter on high ground.

Chapter Thirteen

A LITTLE CLASS

I do not beat my dogs or ambush game wardens, but I am certain now that I shall never be a gentleman sportsman. I once wore a necktie to shoot at some doves, and some years back I bought a tweed jacket with leather shoulder patches, but nothing seemed to work. In a sort of supreme effort at refinement my wife bought me a modest British side-by-side "game gun." It shoots fine, but I really don't feel very different.

This cultural block began in my youth when I was shooting at rabbits in southeastern Kansas, and while I was harmlessly gun crazy as a child I had never heard of Holland & Holland, Boss, or Purdey.

I have studied the proper terminology and I know it is wrong to say I go quail hunting. As our more cultured American sportsmen learned long ago from the mother country, you do not "hunt" birds. Hunting is for big game; you "gun" birds. I try to remember this when I am clawing over Oregon rimrock after chukars, but I can't help feeling that I am hunting. I now have some personal friends who talk to me of "gunning," and I keep trying to use the term myself, but I always choke on it, peering about furtively while imagining that the ghost of some old prairie-chicken banger is listening. I even have trouble using the word "gun" for the shooter at a field trial, though I know the passengers in a plantation wagon are properly "guns" instead of people. Although I am sure no one intends to offend by asking me to go gunning, I feel the same as I do when a restaurant waitress asks me if I "wish a libation from the bar." I am always tempted to say, "No, but I'd like a shot of booze."

I did not encounter the upper crust easterners in a covey until, at an advanced age, I was attached to Admiral Alan Kirk's staff for more than a year during World War II. Kirk believed in the old school tie and had gathered officers from the better families. I came on as a sort of homespun oddity since he needed a photographer and the better folks weren't too long on that craft. Although I couldn't speak the language, I found that the socialite sports tended to be very nice guys.

So this is not derogatory of the cultured hunter (gunner, that is), rather it is a bit of wonderment at his world, which still expands only tentatively west of the Mississippi. All of this is the result of the early concentration of feather shooters in the East, especially the ones who wrote about it and read about it. Of course there have been some treasured southern shotgun writers, but most of the westerners wrote about elk, grizzly bears, and antelope, and considered bird shooting a sort of relaxing offshoot of other hunting. Even now, some of them are short on neckties and tweeds while packing firearms and are unlikely to report "top-hole sport," even though they may carry Purdeys while wearing jeans. For that matter, there are some who call jeans "overalls," a pretty sure sign they have seen quite a patch of sagebrush and disdain the modern term.

I have here a well-done piece about upland ammunition, written by one of my favorite eastern authorities, and he explains there is no need for more than an ounce of shot for upland shooting except for pheasants. This is surprising for those who pull down on seven-pound sage grouse roosters and fifty-yard sharptails. But hardly any of his readers will question his report as most of them consider any game west of the Mississippi to be novelty shooting anyway. To most of them a chukar trip borders on the bizarre, and they really recognize only the big four—ruffed grouse, quail, woodcock, and pheasant. So I see my admired author's side of it.

The English aristocracy, from whom our shooting traditions came, has indeed done more shooting than hunting with its scatterguns. When shooters stand at numbered butts and have game choused to them by beaters it's hard to say they are hunting, and that sport is revered (and followed) by many Americans who can afford it—in Britain, on the European continent, or at home. In this business the guns don't generally manage the retrievers. There's no hiking, no scheming, and not much hardship until the rain starts.

I'm not presuming to grade the shooting sports but they sure do differ. And I never said it's easy to hit a pheasant coming full-bore over a hedge and looking even higher than he is. Some of the greatest British shooters got their reputations in that kind of operation, some of them having stacked up a lot of game, and the number one gun of all time is popularly believed to have been the Earl of Ripon, who tallied more than half a million kills before 1923 and is said to have had "seven pheasants dead in the air at one time."

When he did that I think either the Earl was awfully handy with a repeater or he was flock shooting. If he used the side-by-side doubles he favored and scragged only one bird per shot, he'd have had to use four different guns while pheasant number one was still falling.

I'm sure the highest scores today are made by the dove shooters, a few of whom have killed more than a thousand in a day in Central or South America.

As with many other shotgunners, I want to follow dogs, even mediocre ones, but I guess I'm definitely a hunter instead of a gunner. And although the kind of short-grass snipe hunting I've done lately has no place for a pointer, it sure is hunting.

This instantly relegates me to the shotgun peasantry, and the editor of an outdoor magazine told me he couldn't use a snipe story as snipe hunting isn't an "in" thing. He's right. Stay off those southern snipe flats. It's sloppy ground and hard to get to and snipe are hard to hit, very small, and said by some to be unfit for human consumption. Also, it rains a great deal in that country, and many people think snipe are imaginary creatures like unicorns.

In solitary brooding I have never been able to learn why sharp-tailed grouse are not as good as woodcock, and for that matter I think Mearns quail compare pretty favorably with bobwhites, even though they do not adapt well to bird wagons and horseback hunters. The running desert quails have their own thing, tough for a dog to hold and often living in rather pugnacious country. None of these have the status of the bobwhite, of course, even though they have been present all the time. Cow pasture just lacks the tradition of cotton and coon country.

Strange is the status of sharptail and true prairie chickens. For generations the trainers of southern super dogs have spent summers in Canada to train their hotshots on young sharptails, but come hunting season they generally pack up to go back south, and they warn me that mature sharptails ruin good dogs.

The chukar, accepted as driven in Europe and Asia, is pretty well ignored by traditional upland shooters in this country except as he is found fat and innocent on preserves. No discredit to those released models, but a shooter of preserve chukars will have to start over when he hears cackling on the face of an Idaho mountain.

Some people with worn boots and snagged pants simply don't believe in preserve hunting, but many traditional gunners do more of that than anything else. Preserve shooting ranges all the way from barnyard performances to something very close to wild game. It depends on the way the birds are produced, and I have seen some quail that flew as hard, as fast, and as far as wild ones did. If a covey hadn't split up immediately after a rise I wouldn't have known whether they had ever seen feeders or wire. However beautiful the scenery or exhilarating the fall breezes, not everyone is pleased by a full day of hard hunting with few chances or no shots at all. Preserves are here to stay.

It is easy for a lover of the true sporting life to feel a bit cool toward a shotgunning peasant who thinks the only reason for owning a best-grade side-by-side is his inability to afford an autoloader. Nowhere is the old school tie so neatly knotted as in the choice of guns, and while I am the product of a rusty single-shot background, even I have been jolted by the coarse attitude of some common folk.

For a very brief period I possessed a really fine British shotgun, probably assembled by a guy who had worn a hole in the floor at his bench. As soon as I got it I clutched it to my palpitating bosom and rushed to the insurance office. They had explained on the phone that they had to see any shotgun worth that kind of money. They looked it up and admired it, but as I left I realized they felt it was purely an antique and they wondered if it would shoot.

Love for sleek side-by-sides is an acquired taste, and while I carry one quite a bit, I am haunted by the suspicion that an over-under might be more efficient. Secretly, I am not even convinced that the pistol grip is useless, and I cannot forget that those who shoot for money, trophies, and glory have largely forsaken both the side-by-side and the straight grip.

I canvassed the gunracks at a big skeet shoot and found, as I already anticipated, that there were no side-by-side guns at all. But then, there are very few Rolls Royces on the stock car racing circuits.

Chapter Fourteen

MYSTICISM AND THE ART OF SHOTGUNNING

I know a lot about shotgun shooting, and I think I would be a wonderful instructor if I were a good shot. I have read a long shelf of shotgun-shooting texts, and I have been coached by some of the best in the business. Instructors like to help me with my shooting because any true master likes a challenge. As a result of this study I am remarkably able to tell why I missed a shot and, in fact, can go into detailed analysis of it. I greatly admire famous shotgun instructors. They deal in mysticism and mental telepathy.

For example, a good shot telephoned an instructor who had once straightened him out from a shooting slump.

"I can't hit at all," he quavered. "I have been knocking off quail and woodcock all fall, and now I go pheasant hunting and the dogs hold them so they get up right under my feet and they cackle and flap and I miss them. Do you think I need a different stock for pheasants?"

"You're not keeping your head down," the instructor said. "I can tell from here."

When somebody straightens out a misser from two thousand miles over a telephone wire, I am interested in just what form of occult information he is dealing in.

"That was easy," the expert said. "If he hadn't lost his glasses or gotten his feet crossed, it almost had to be that he wasn't getting his head down. This guy had been nailing little quail that went off like bumblebees and little woodcock that had to be stopped short of the willows, so he did everything right. Then a pheasant rooster gets up like a Christmas goose four feet away, and it's so easy he just points in the general direction and misses twice."

Now, of course, it is carved somewhere on a rock that lifting your head is the expert's miss, but often nothing short of a slow-motion video will prove to the average shooter that he doesn't have his head down. Keeping your head down is one of the first rules, but I know a pretty fair shooter who wrote a good book on skeet and didn't go into detail on that part at all. I asked him why he didn't emphasize that part. He lowered his voice.

"I never have put my head down," he said. "I just point the damned thing. That's why I don't care if the pull is seventeen inches or twelve, and I am not going to write about something I don't know anything about."

I think this proves shotgunning is partly supernatural.

Poor shotgun pointers are psychos, but then good shotgun pointers are psychos, too. Despite a personal effort at avoiding such situations, I found myself stuck with one of the best of bobwhite shooters. Except for being a shotgun wizard he was a very nice guy and pretended not to notice if I fumbled the safety or stopped my gun as a quail passed a tree trunk. We were at a pretty classy quail resort where the dogs were glossy and I didn't have the right clothes for dinner.

Anyway, my friend killed quail effortlessly and modestly, and when we came back to the clubhouse I noticed a well-designed practice trap layout with several gunners whanging away. It had been designed specifically to help quail shooters, and a British-looking man in a tweed shooting jacket and one of those snap-down visor caps was coaching them. As we went by the practice setup, my ordinarily graceful friend seemed to have trouble walking, and I noted he was trying to proceed sideways, facing away from the trap.

"Don't look at those damn clay targets!" he hissed. "They'll ruin your bird shooting!"

Before you attribute this comment to a superstitious peasant, I should mention that he was about the most highly cultured business success I know of, and he'd picked a pretty good university in his youth. He shot birds all over the world, using the appropriate shotguns with tasteful engraving.

But then, there was something else I should get in here. The man who didn't like to look at clay pigeons hunted in a ragged old vest I wouldn't dry off my dog with. He said new vests were bad luck and sort of bound him across the shoulders or something.

Now most shotgun instructors do their thing with clay targets of one kind or another, and the sporting clays game will keep you modest, even if you smear the easy ones. Unless you have an inexhaustible supply of live birds stomping around your place, chances are any instruction you get will be done with clays.

I had an old fishing friend who had simply gotten away from bird shooting for a long time. I knew he had been a hunter in his youth, and he wanted to try it again. We went to see a trap and skeet champion who ran a gun club, and my friend tried his best, but couldn't seem to hit anything. The club operator really went to work with him, but the results weren't too good. He finally shook his head and said it was going to take a lot of practice.

"It's just what I figured," old Les said. "My eyes are gone and my glasses don't help much. I just can't see what I'm doing. Sometimes I see two or three of those things and sometimes I don't see any at all."

I gently suggested that Les might take up golf, but he said he was too old for that and probably wouldn't be able to tell where his ball went anyway. He said he hadn't shot any doves for a long time, and he thought he'd go to a dove shoot.

Since he hadn't been able to hit a slow clay target going straight away, I figured the doves were pretty safe. But it didn't work out like that. Les swung his old pumpgun with the solid rib, and doves dropped with impressive regularity. I asked him how he could hit doves when the same clay target would last him all afternoon.

"Aw, doves are different," he said. "They wiggle their wings."

Real shotgun instructors, who work with people who have burned a lot of powder in the past, acquire some extrasensory perception. I used to hunt snipe with J.D., who was one of those perfectionists who can't even eat his lunch if he has missed three shots in a row. Where snipe are concerned I can't afford to let my inaccuracy starve me to death. Unwilling to admit that long-range snipe over short grass had his number, J.D. went to a professional instructor, and he looked pretty bad to begin with. The instructor told him to try it with both eyes open. At first, that wasn't easy for J.D. after all those years, but he decided it helped.

"How did he know I shut one eye?" J.D. wondered. "He was standing behind me all the time. He's an Englishman. Does that have something to do with it?"

In Britain, where not every male child is born a deadly shotgun pointer, it was natural for the shooting school to be developed. And, of course, when someone pays the price of a house and lot to get a British side-by-side shotgun, he has some additional incentive to learn what to do with it. So the shooting school and the shooting instructor developed fast in England, and some of the teachers came to the colonies where there were things like autoloaders, and even some fairly literate citizens who had never had pheasants driven over their heads, being addicted to "rough shooting."

Well, the British instructors certainly had individual ideas, but the main thing was that you point the shotgun with your left hand and you forgo the frontier style of "aiming" over a barrel. They had us holding our left hands way out there past the fore-end, which they avoided as much as possible, and leather hand-guards protected the barrels from your damp hand and protected your hand from the hot barrels. Some enterprising stockmakers built some extra-long fore-ends to solve that problem, but they didn't have the classic look and connoisseurs of British weaponry criticized them darkly and even mentioned the word "pumpgun" under their breath.

The British system is a little like instinct shooting, as taught by some American experts, and the main thing is to keep your eyes focused on the target and let the barrel take care of itself while you point with the hand that holds it.

Now and then there are complications for some individuals. I have an excellent background in shotgunnery, having tried all of the wrong ways at one time or another. When I first concluded it really was better not to aim a shotgun, I began to get with the business of really keeping my head down for an instant after each shot so I could check and prove if I had done everything right. I had been doing this for quite a while when I went into a sort of super slump in which I missed all sorts of birds that appeared to be laughing as they passed me. I believe the laughing part may have been partly my imagination.

I rushed to an expert and told him with a quivering lip that I was doing everything right and that, as I looked over the barrel after shooting, with the gun still in place, the bird tended to continue on its course. So I fired a few shots at targets as he watched.

"The drill is to move the gun up behind the target while you are mounting it," he said, "and as you catch the bird you seat the stock and fire as you swing through. Then you can hold the gun in position and check if it was pointed right. But you're shooting before you ever get it to your shoulder, and then after you finally do get it there you check very carefully to see how you think it was pointed."

I did much better after that, but I resented the fact that he yawned while he told me what was wrong.

There was a good shot who hadn't gone too far in science and said there was no need to lead anything. His argument was that if you fastened a long string to a weight and swung it around you, the string always pointed at the weight no matter how fast it went.

"Don't tell him shooting is different," one of his friends said. "As long as he hits, he doesn't need to know he's leading, and if you tell him he'll start missing and have a nervous breakdown."

Charlie is a good wingshot but says his shooting was ruined by his father, who told him to concentrate on the barrel and bead and aim carefully. I told him it was too bad his father didn't know any better and started him wrong.

"Yeah," he said, "but Dad was the best quail shot in the county."

I went to Fred Missildine's shooting school. Missildine had been a famous competitive shotgunner for a long time and did years of championship skeet with Winchester pumpguns. I heard he had taught in Europe, which surprised me as I thought shooting instructors always came across the Atlantic in the other direction. Maybe they wanted him because he looked so sharp in his shooting jacket. Anyway, I was in awe of Fred Missildine, who seemed to have some sort of friendly control over his students. This is a common characteristic of elite shooting coaches.

I first heard about Missildine's instruction from a newspaperman who went to see how he worked and had no shotgun experience at all. He said Missildine took him out to a skeet range, stood behind him, and began telling him how to fire each individual station. He said that starting from scratch he hadn't missed any at all, figured he had the word, and there was nothing much to it. Then he suddenly started missing, and when he turned to ask for help Missildine was gone, having been called to the telephone. He spoke of this in hushed tones.

Since I asked about game shooting instead of competition, Missildine worked out targets to give me a variety of approaches, telling me the drill for each one.

Flinching is something done in a variety of ways, of course, ranging from a slight fudge to an inability to make the gun fire at all. If I try to change results by thinking about too many things at once, I'll sometimes fudge a little. I mentioned this, whereupon Missildine told me firmly that he would put up with no flinching at all. A few minutes later, trying to correct all of my faults at once, I jerked the gun and missed. Nothing happened so I turned slowly. My mentor had turned his back to me, walked away, and was staring off across a marsh. Finally, he took a deep breath, came back, and started over. I didn't flinch again.

Truly scientific innovators like me work out all sorts of methods for assuring hits on all kinds of game. Shivering in a skimpy duck blind with mallards coming and going through a snowstorm, I found myself shooting behind them and sought a method of correction. If I'd just tell myself to swing faster and farther every time, things would work out better, I figured. So I told myself, "P-u-s-h-!" each time, and I shot better. Much later, a friend said he thought he was shooting behind his birds, and I revealed my technical secret. Next time I saw him, he was very thankful and asked me where I learned what to do.

I assume this makes me a top-rank expert. Should I start a school?

Chapter Fifteen

MEAT DOGS AND CHAMPIONS

The best bird dog I ever knew flunked the only field trial he entered, but if nobody ever kept score somewhere we'd be hunting with some strange livestock.

To prove that you're a real sport of the old school and that you scorn the pedigreed hotshots, it's very convincing to use the old pronouncement: "I haven't shot a bird over a piece of paper yet." I, too, have slandered the blue bloods of dogdom from time to time, usually when I have just seen a perfect performance by a bedraggled mutt from nowhere, who might have ended up in the pound instead of the brush patches.

They used to say the modern automobile was developed on the world's racetracks, and there's a lot to that, although I wouldn't want to head for the supermarket with one of those Indianapolis screamers, or a dragster that can barely keep its front wheels on the ground. For the most part, the breeders and the field trialers have done themselves proud.

The very business of pointing birds as a favor to somebody with a gun is a pretty good trick, built in by centuries of training and selection. Breaking that little group into fast workers, slow workers, wide rangers, close workers, dead hunters, and retrievers has taken quite a few generations.

But I have owned a bird dog that I couldn't catch, one that insisted on riding in somebody else's truck, and one that would hide a dead bird after pointing it for me to shoot. These things indicate that even a glowing pedigree on double-weight parchment may not have all the answers, and each one of these weirdos had some kind of a champion in its family tree and was pretty to look at.

I wouldn't advise buying any dog purely by what its papers say, but they sure make important reading. The main thing here is to remember that the farther back you get into Fido's ancestry, the less important the big names are, and that his papa and mama count the most. At the same time, if you're getting a pup to wriggle through the willows and aspen after ruffed grouse, you should be a bit wary of those names that indicate barn burners who ran the judges' horses into a lather in long-ago field trials. Maybe some of those genes will surface, causing the family pet to get up from the fireplace and leave you wondering where he went.

I speak not from a career of top-notch gun dogs, but as one who has blown it on numerous occasions and considers the purchase of a bird dog a decision worthy of deep study and considerable soul-searching. Bird-dog buying should be on a worry level of about nine, akin to house buying and marriage. Few shotgunners take it that seriously—at first.

The most risky dog purchase is of a freshly weaned puppy, complicated by the fact that all puppies are cute. When chosen from a litter, a pup is picked for several reasons, such as being the prettiest, ugliest, smallest, largest, boldest, or shyest of the bunch. But it isn't a frivolous decision. After a pup reaches hunting age he is likely to be so firmly entrenched in the family scene that he won't be discarded, even if he can't find his own dish. The shooters of the family are doomed to his presence for his lifetime.

The most economical way of getting a good productive bird dog is to buy a fairly young one who has been trained and shot over and has given a good account of himself...on the new owner's kind of birds. Since few will pay any attention to this advice, I put it in here to please myself. Such a dog seems expensive—at first.

Enter now the field-trial business. It is in field trials of one kind or another that champion gun dogs are rated. The key words here are "of one kind or another." Best known of the trophy takers are those who win in the open type of trial, where the judges and handlers ride pretty good horses in most cases. This kind of champion points and is steady to shot. He does not hunt dead and he does not retrieve. The typical brushpatch foot hunter would be about as well off with a racing dromedary.

What ruins this reasoning is the fact that some of those horizon scratchers can settle down and spend a long day with a slow walker and a heavy shotgun. They are exceptions so don't expect it.

One of the wildest gambles a foot hunter can take is to buy a pup a year or so old that has been discarded by people seeking open-age field-trial dogs and who have decided the youngster won't cut it with cowboy handlers and horseback galleries. I have tried that kind of dog twice and am an authority on the subject. The wrong genes popped up in my treasures. I do not own a horse.

About two long jumps behind the open field-trialer is the "shooting dog," as used by operators of quail plantations. There are special trials for him, too, but when at work back on the plantation he doesn't bother to hunt dead or follow cripples. They pull him away from such errant tendencies and send him for a new covey. There are retrievers on the wagon.

For many years there have been shoot-to-retrieve trials, favoring fairly close-working dogs that were expected to retrieve after going through all of the other formalities. A winner at this kind of trial (which is becoming more and more popular) will fit right into the foot hunter's plans but probably isn't for sale. A puppy or started dog from this corner is probably pretty controllable, regardless of pointing breed. Control is always nice but becomes essential when you're barely balanced on a steep talus slope and would rather your dog did not point chukars somewhere around the mountain where you will be seeking him in moonlight, or even rain.

There used to be concise hunters' descriptions for the various breeds. The English pointer acquired a reputation for being a bird-finding machine with only disdain for the wife and kids. The English setter was a little more social and generally didn't run quite as far or as fast but looked pretty beside a fireplace. The Brittany spaniel was described as the "old man's dog" and was supposed to hunt in your shadow on hot days. The German shorthair was a plodder who specialized in pointing pheasants eye-to-eye—and so on.

But these divisions have faded considerably with all sorts of breeding experiments, some of which produced just strange-looking dogs, and some of which produced super-hunters. Some of the Brittanies grew longer legs that seldom touched the ground. Some of the English pointers slowed down to a sedate trot, and some setters took on weight and tippytoed through the brush after ruffs. Some of the shorthairs dropped into another gear, and there was one shorthair breeder who said, "Dock their tails quick before they become English pointers!"

Dogs can be converted from one kind of hunting to another—sometimes, depending on intelligence or lack of it. Like humans, they have different kinds of smarts. A concert pianist may be a mite slow on calculus.

One of the "smartest" bird dogs I ever owned was an English pointer who adapted to different kinds of game, could be trained almost instantly regarding where to sit or lie in somebody else's vehicle, and seemed to know exactly how close she could get to any variety of game bird without flushing it—but never learned how to roll in or on anything. While other dogs managed to come in happily stinking from contact with some undesirable object found afield, she was never able to hit the target and made my story really good when she tried to roll on a long-dead cow and missed. Completely true.

When she put her nose down and began to roll, she never learned where the rest of her would end up.

I have known dogs from big-going strains that would heel or sit at a soft-spoken request, that were perfect house pets and would stay in the kennel with the door open if you told them to—but which became completely uncontrollable specks on distant hillsides when they hit the ground in game country. The point is that anything desirable you can get through breeding gives you a head start.

No real red-blooded sport will admit he knows nothing about bird dogs. I knew a prosperous foot hunter who operated in pheasant country most of the time but also pursued sharp-tailed grouse in the high grasslands of the West. He mentioned to me that he had bought two dogs from distant kennels and had to send both of them back. The dogs came from close-working German shorthair stock with a good reputation, and I wondered.

"I couldn't do anything with either of them," he said. "They'd get out there forty or fifty yards, and anybody knows you can't hit birds that take off that far away."

I stood there a little dazed, suddenly realizing the man didn't even know what pointing dogs were for. He had been brought up on well-trained Labrador flushing dogs, which certainly have their place but have different kinds of parents. He thought a pointing dog could hold a bird for only a few seconds.

My worst blunders have involved true big-going, open field-trial stock. In my infinite wisdom I reasoned that I could take a young "started" dog and adjust his range to my needs, even if his ancestors had been running big-time field trials for a dozen generations. His pedigree read like a who's who, but the breeder said he didn't range far enough. I'll go to the next paragraph in a minute but I am getting shaky again as I look back on that scene.

When I went to the big kennel to pick out my dog, they had several youngsters from which to choose. They put long check cords on them and turned them loose in a well-fenced pasture. The whole bunch left in a shower of sand except for one who showed no sign of wanting to hunt. I rejected him.

"They're full of pep," the kennel owner said, "but they just won't run wide enough for trial operations."

He was sincere. I bought the only one we could catch and spent a couple of seasons looking for him on distant ridges and in other people's kennels. With ardent training I may have shortened his range a few feet, but when he was half a mile away and opening that was hardly noticeable. For benefit of the experience, I put him with a professional trainer for a couple of months, and the professional worked him hard, regretfully took my money, admired his stamina, and said I might as well have an Airdale.

But that was not my most colorful experience with dogs not intended for foot hunting. Some folks in the horseback field-trial business were closing out their operation and had a lantern-jawed pointer, a year old, who had never been in the field but who came from a strain of winners. Here, I thought, was the perfect foil for my perceptive training approaches. I could start with a dog with an open mind—produce anything I wanted from a dog who had gotten past most of his puppyhood and was ready to receive the truth.

My friends are sick of hearing my story of what followed, but it perfectly illustrates the field-trial mystique as related to meat dogs followed by pedestrians. The name of our subject appeared as Magnificent Murphy on his pedigree, although I habitually referred to him in other terms.

I tried to follow him, but he always disappeared. However, unlike most such supercharged explorers, Murphy would stop and yell for help when he felt he was hopelessly lost. I do not recall shooting any birds over him, and he once ran up a measured eighty acres of sage grouse without stopping for breath, after which he sat down atop a haystack. This penchant for haystacks grew from some early training programs that had involved hay—in bales. To Murph, bales and stacks were about the same.

He didn't point often but when he did, he meant it. Once he came down hard on a covey of Hungarian partridge, showing all the style his ancestors demanded. The Huns had left the vicinity and finally took off about two hundred yards away. Murph never moved a muscle so I tried to talk him into breaking his point, which I finally accomplished with a couple of firm tugs on his collar.

He ate his full share of dog food and demanded just as many comforts as dogs over which I shot birds. One amateur trainer asked for an opportunity to train him, but that did not work out. Murphy left, dragging part of his new kennel with him. He did not come home to me; he just trotted off on a main street. He trotted instead of running because the part of the kennel he had pulled loose with his chain was quite heavy.

Now to the point of my oft-repeated story. I forced Murphy on a professional trainer who handled field-trial dogs. It was a gift and the only stipulation was that I never see Murphy again. I never did, but I saw his picture in *The American Field* when he won a national chicken championship in Canada. You see, there was a niche for Murph, but it wasn't in my kind of hunting. Many very good professional boxers have shown little aptitude for space science.

The term "meat dog" is short on glamour but often means a good hunter who is a bit weak on class. But a dog who never won a field trial of any kind can have a classy appearance, and the best meat dogs are seldom for sale. And back there somewhere, almost everybody's dog has been affected by field trials.

Chapter Sixteen

LOST DOGS

While the man at the Wyoming service station was fixing our water pump a beautiful Brittany came past, wagged his tail at the filling station operator, and trotted toward the nearby house. I asked the man if the dog was a good hunter and he grinned.

"Oh, I don't hunt," the man said. "That dog's just passing through. Stopped off six years ago."

There are gypsy dogs who see the country, there are wild dogs who have felt the pull of their wolfish ancestors, and there are lost dogs, some of them tragically afraid in an unknown world of fearsome strangers and mysterious terrors. And there are owners ranging from professionals, who run dozens of hunting dogs and accept an occasional loss as a sad part of the game, to weeping youngsters whose world has collapsed.

Dog stories become fables, although the truth is often stranger than the fiction. There is the recurrent tale of dogs who come home from incredible distances, and there are equally poignant stories of dogs who have waited through starvation for masters who may have gone forever. Dog stories tend to be emotional, and when I became hooked on the pointing breeds and their human-instilled instincts (did you ever really think of what is involved in finding and pointing a bird while waiting an hour for a shooter?) I was fascinated by lost dogs, the wonder of their noses, their incredible intelligence and their incredible stupidity. A great many bird dogs are lost because we have extended their ranges and bred the drive into them. Trailing hounds are lost because of their single purpose that overcomes even their survival instincts. But this is not a learned discourse on dog training or handling. I guess it is just a gee-whiz comment on lost dog wonders, and I begin with the Afghan and the trip to Bermuda.

There is a freeway (I-90) that passes Bozeman, Montana, and we follow it part way to the airport at Belgrade, following it as it swings around Bozeman with a couple of exits there. The Afghan was at the east exit when I first saw it, standing at the side of the road as if expecting a car to stop and pick it up. The Afghan is regal enough to get attention and this one was showy, even to a bird-dog man.

It was two weeks later that I saw the Afghan again. It was at the same spot on the interstate, and although its coat remained glossy it was thin and I suspected it might be lost. Now I don't know why Bermuda becomes important, but that was the year we went there, the year the dog stayed by a highway overpass while we went fishing thousands of miles away.

Back from Bermuda, we were driving past Bozeman from the airport when my wife Debie and I saw the Afghan beside the road, emaciated and ragged, trying to eat something—a bit of trash that had some scent of food. So I stopped the car and tried to get near it but it ran under the overpass just a few yards away, going with the shambling gait of weakness. Although I could not get near it we left some dog food at its station and I called the Bozeman animal shelter, where they said they'd had a report of a lost Afghan. I haven't seen the dog since so I suppose it finally met whomever it was waiting for—after at least six weeks.

Wide-ranging trailing hounds, they of the "cold" noses, are lost by thousands each hunting season, most of them getting back some way. I have hunted in a national forest where deer dogs are used and have met them in varied stages of suffering, some of them trying to climb into my truck, and some of them slipping into trailside brush. I have walked up to a pointing dog that acted a little strangely and found him pointing a prone Walker hound that had finally given up and was barely alive in a patch of weeds.

It is scent that brings lost dogs home, we're sure, and it is the enormous memory banks of canine scent we will never understand, no matter how many laboratories and computers examine them. It is this other world of smell that enables a retrieving pointer to hold a dead bird in its mouth and point a live one twenty feet away, and the matter is so awesome that old dog trainers change the subject after brief discussion. When a dog finds its way home from considerable distance it is usually scent that makes it possible, but unless he follows his own trail the chances are that it will take a long while—a period in which he catches the general scent of his home area, the more specific scent of his community—and then his exact doorstep by the elimination of thousands of distracting scent trails.

You will note that I am waxing authoritative on something I know no more about than anyone else who has greeted a bedraggled wanderer after giving him up. It is simply that I spend much of my time writing about and watching hunting dogs and have thus acquired bravado on the subject. I have watched a tired dog perk up—after three thousand miles in a car—twenty miles from home, jump up and down five miles from home, and start barking while a mile away.

Now I have heard learned explanations of scent and its distribution, and dogs have been able to find everything from lost eyeglasses to heroin, but some of the failures are as spectacular as the triumphs. Three of us hunted on a snowy hillside for ruffed grouse—an area of patchy woods and open parks—and we were using two old veterans of the country, good Brittany buddies who approached the project with slavering conniving and sly looks. It was not a strange hillside for them, but they would become lost within minutes and need to be tracked down. One of them, completely confused, stood and barked for help. After each had become lost twice we took them off the hill. The scent had failed them, even though snow is not generally a deterrent.

The general rule is that very dry weather is bad for scenting, heat is derogatory, and rain washes scent away, but there are those days when a usually reliable dog stands with a foot inches from a dead bird and stares at his master for instructions—the same dog who homed in on a kill from fifty feet the day before. It is when the scent doesn't work right that dogs are lost, and little is said generally of the wanderers who are searched for after most of the big field trials.

There is the old trick so often employed by hound users. Leave a piece of your clothing near where you last saw the fugitive and come back the next day. Thousands of dogs have been found lying beside a shirt or jacket, but the part we don't know is how many miles they traveled in the general area before they caught the familiar scent. It becomes eerie.

Old Spike disappeared in a Florida forest—hundreds of square miles of piney woods, wiregrass, palmetto, and scrub oak. Spike, a Brittany old enough to know better, had been lost before, being a careless wanderer not above following a deer briefly if no one was watching. I last heard his bell early in the afternoon, and late that night Debie and I were on the scene with the truck lights on and making all the noise we could—firing the usual shotgun blasts and driving the sand roads for miles near where he had disappeared. We also commented on Spike's general character and tried to tell ourselves it was good riddance. We posted a bulletin board message at the nearest country store, and it was shortly after that it began to rain—hard.

"There goes the scent he'd have to follow," I said. "The old fool would have barely enough sense to backtrail himself *with* it. Now he's really a goner and we'll have to wait for someone to read his tag and get in touch."

None of this is fun, but humans did it to themselves when they taught pointing dogs to range—and range still farther. Some ransoms for lost dogs are pretty steep.

"We'll put out the dog box from the truck," Debie said, "and I'll fix a pan of dog food and a pan of water. Then you can check tomorrow morning."

Like flowers at a funeral I felt it would accomplish no particular good for the subject but helped set out the dog box and Debie fixed the pans. The whole works was set at the edge of a timber patch where I'd last heard old Spike's bell. I explained to Debie the slim chance of his coming that way, but most of the trip home was pretty quiet. It always is when there's a dog gone—unless you try to cover up the pall that has descended.

It was long before daylight when I stuck the headlight beams into the woods again, and before I took to some more sand roads I started to drive past the dog box, knowing the pans of food and water would be a rather pathetic scene. But Spike was there, and although the food had been eaten he was a quivering, cowering little wretch, somewhat afraid of me. He did not get lost again, and it may be he had tasted the true ashes of terror. Most hunting dogs are not equipped for survival on their own. One seldom-realized fact is the distance a dog travels in an hour, and the thought that one might have gone a hundred miles in twelve hours is staggering. Watch a healthy bird finder on the move. A hundred miles? A thousand checks of places that look right or smell just a little bit right? And is there some special instinct beyond scent and eyesight? A guiding hand?

There are unexplained losses. There was the time I misplaced two pointing dogs at once in a series of ridges and ledges, one of them wearing an electronic beeper and the other a bell. Two hours later I could hear both beeper and bell from different directions but no amplified whistle or gunshot could bring them nearer. I finally ran down both dogs, finding them confused and glad to see me, and my analysis is that they had considered the situation so simple they ignored their backtrails and were confused by echoes. I don't know when I have been so tired.

Cold trails? Perhaps it is the bloodhound who is best on them, but an English pointer can follow one hours old as a routine matter. I have no doubt the retrievers can do the same but they seldom have the occasion to. My old English pointer disappeared on a mountain in scattered snow. We had found no birds and I suspected she had, for once, abandoned me and gone "self-hunting," as the trainers say. It was still early in the day when I gave up and went home for help and long-suffering Debie was left with the truck near where I had started walking that morning. She had a binocular view of a nearly bare mountainside, more than half a mile of unobstructed grass, rocks, and snow. She had parked on a little ridge for a better view of the spot I had left from early that day and at dusk she saw a speeding speck that grew into the pointer at top speed and the racer slid to a stop where the truck had been parked that morning.

There are certain conditions that seem to destroy any scent, and I suspect that the truly lost dog simply encounters a stretch of his back track that carries nothing to smell. The really top hounds will cut wide circles to pick up a trail again. Perhaps many bird dogs lack that finesse.

Some expert fox hunters showed me how hard it was for their Walkers and Black and Tans to trail across pavement or on plowed ground. I once found it impossible to keep track of a dog that was continually lost in brush somewhere beside an old abandoned asphalt road I was walking on. I had been hunting in swampy land and was wearing rubber boots, and it finally soaked in that the dog simply could not trail me on the hot asphalt but was not wise enough to recognize his problem and kept running off into the brush, circling behind me and getting lost. Finally, I put him on a lead.

Probably worst of all are the bird dogs that trail deer, a strange phenomenon of breeding that somehow has retained the wrong hunting instincts. Such dogs may starve, and they may be lost for a week or forever, unable to resist the urge they have been taught is wrong. Some true addicts never change.

Wanderer, fumbler, self-hunter, ancestor worshiper. Genes from ancient blood. Have the breeders really won?

Chapter Seventeen

PLENTY OF
RIFLES

I shot through a tree with a .30-40 Krag-Jorgensen rifle. It was a surprisingly large tree, but the hole was very small as the bullet was metal-jacketed for military use.

The hole where the bullet came out was so small I suspected it might have been made by a worm, so I shot through the tree again. The elm was as logical a target as any, since Kansas at that time was a little short on any game larger than the rare coyote sighted across the draw south of our barn.

Lacking advanced ballistic information at that time, and assuming penetration was the ultimate gauge of killing power, I felt the Krag was a super rifle. It was left over from the Spanish-American War, with only the issue bayonet missing.

Feelings about rifle calibers have cemented and broken friendships. For example, a catchy name will overpower all sorts of statistics gained by chronometers or laboratories. The .30-30 Winchester, which has been around since 1895, really began to fade as a big-game rifle only a few years back. Hollywood and the businesslike "thutty-thutty" name kept it in the back of pickup trucks and slung to Western saddles long after dozens of better cartridges were developed— and forgotten.

When Winchester introduced the now highly respected .243 in 1955, I got one dressed up by famous gunsmith Bob Chow in San Francisco. Shortly afterward, I found myself soft-walking down a mountainside above Jack Creek near Ennis, Montana. With me, and off to one side, was a local resident who had promised to show me a buck as we came down upon bedding sites in early morning. He stopped and pointed downward at a bedded deer. I carefully took a solid position and was placing the crosshairs when he hissed uncertainty into my ear.

"That thing may not do it!" he said. "You wanta use this?"

My Montana friend, of course, was offering me his .270, which was known to have a rapport with western game, largely through the literary works of Jack O'Connor, famous *Outdoor Life* gun editor, who had used it far and wide, and who had a large and worshipful readership. Did I have a trace of doubt myself?

The .243 killed the buck all right. There are now some shiny and attractive homes where we found him. Getting him down the mountain was mainly a matter of following where he slid.

Now and then I get calls from people who have read some of the yellowed pages on which I once recorded great truths about guns. One asked me the other day what would be the best all-around big- and medium-game rifle. I started to say the .280 was my choice, but then I thought he might want heavy bullets for big bears and told him the .30-06 was hard to equal. Since it has been around for eighty-seven years, I didn't feel I was reporting anything new. I hope I won't offend lovers of big bullets, as in the .45-70, or worshipers of velocity who might prefer the .257 Weatherby.

The .45-70 fell in with U.S. Army ranks around 1873 and went West to meet hostile Indians. A thousand paintings and sketches show the old high-hammered trapdoor singleshots in battle, used by men of another age on a mission of bloody subjugation.

Later generations called such rifles "punkin rollers" for their slow, heavy bullets, and there have been times when the high-velocity lovers have made fun of them. However, not long ago I walked with an Alaska fishing guide who carried a stubby, customized lever-action Marlin .45-70 as a bear deterrent. I hear the word "revival" regarding the .45-70.

I was fooling with rifles when the wildcatters became the wildest, and I would often meet them on weedy old rifle ranges and in backcountry coulees where they set up homemade bench rests and stared down-range with wild expressions. Sometimes I left briskly. Years later, there were affordable chronograph rigs for experimenters, but some of those early operators went by muzzle blast, recoil, and whether or not they could open the gun after firing an experimental load. Velocity was the goal of most, and one I encountered was having difficulty: the bullet never made it to the target because it was blowing up in the air. This was not extremely rare but I mention it for the benefit of souls who have led protected lives and have not heard of such things.

At one time there was a minor passion for the "bull-pup" rifle, which was built with the breech back by the shooter's ear, making the whole thing very short. This would be very convenient as carry-on luggage or for walking through slit trenches, and a few of them are still being put together by clever gunsmiths with time on their hands. However, one shooter, who dealt with freestyle wildcats, vetoed the idea, saying that when the thing blew up he didn't want it back by his ear.

Roy Weatherby, who really merchandised the fast ones, had suitable rifles, of course, and he sold high velocity until lovers of it rushed to gunshops drooling slightly.

Weatherby was right when he figured anyone who wanted a real smoker like one of his rifles would like to have it show.

So he produced fancy stocks of exotic wood with fancy inlays. It is not true they lit up but you could sure see them coming. Checkering was ornate.

Then there were the lovers of "traditional" gunstocks, who were willing to pay long prices for deeply figured walnut that came from exotic places where very old trees curled up for lack of water, but which must be carved into accepted shapes. This was a cult of conservatives who hardly ever painted flames on their sedans. The classic stock has a refined beauty, of course, and its lovers inspect the checkering with magnifying glasses. Restrained engraving is accepted. Ideally, it shouldn't be too perfect, I guess, because any handwork will show tiny imperfections treasured by the faithful.

Now Jack O'Connor, strong on the conservative side, liked a skeleton buttplate on his custom rifles. Only recently, a sacrilegious Johnny-come-lately mentioned that he liked a pad to soak up the recoil and another infidel said a steel buttplate makes a hell of a click when it bumps a rock. Although I treasured O'Connor's word, I never had a steel buttplate and I don't think O'Connor would object.

Not only do certain cartridges catch on while others are forgotten, but some of the best have a tough time getting established, if they ever do. Winchester's .270 has been a tough one to bypass, and when Remington came up with the .280 it took a hard sell to start it. The .280 is a 7 mm cartridge and a near duplicate of cartridges most people never heard of. Remington had learned long ago that the word "millimeter" paralyzed American sales.

When the Remington .280 rifle appeared, I studied the ballistics and bought two of them—one for my wife (when I get sold, I'm overboard). I took mine into a camp of deer and elk hunters, who viewed me with sympathy. They assumed I either couldn't afford a .270 or simply didn't understand, and although the .280 worked fine, they were never sold. Remington had a tough time with their new rifle and soon discontinued it in the bolt model. After that, I did some snooping and, as far as I can tell, the .280 was the number one caliber for custom rifles almost immediately. The .280 isn't magic. It's just a good caliber that works in a fairly light, short rifle and continues in ups and downs.

Even some ardent hunters who wear good boots, work hard, and study game animals almost to the point of invasion of privacy have fanciful ideas about rifles and their cartridges. One of them had a rifle breakdown just before deer season opened and borrowed one from me, insisting on buying ammunition. He sighted-in briefly and, being a good shot, promptly bagged a big mule deer buck and an antelope but said he'd be glad to get his old .30-06 back. My rifle was a .280. He had bought varmint ammo.

Being a new member of a true caliber cult can be dangerous. When one prosperous believer in super calibers was ready to take a trip into grizzly bear country, he wanted me to help him sight in his new whizzer, which would handle anything that walks if it were pointed properly. As I expected when I approached the benchrest, it bellowed and kicked fearsomely and its owner said he wanted me to do most of the shooting as he had faith in my ability. After being belted a few times by a rather strange stock and beginning to develop a spectacular flinch, as well as a nervous tic, I found that only about half of the cartridges would fire. There was no time to get new ones and I urgently suggested that the temperamental combination should never be carried within range of even a small grizzly bear. Did he have another rifle?

Oh, yes, he had a faithful old .30-06, but was taking his new Whiz-Banger for safety's sake. Since the 30.-06 (with appropriate bullets) has been flattening grizzlies for several generations, I mentioned that an ordinary rifle that goes off regularly would be better than a cannon that only clicks about half the time. I also suggested that if he used his sometime devastator, he should get a bayonet mounted on it. I added that Russian roulette is said to be an exciting sport too. He was lucky. He found no grizzlies.

I have no fringed leather pants, but maybe the blackpowder rifle lovers bear watching, having passed up the fads and foibles of recent years. The old buffalo guns threw great chunks of lead for very long distances, leading to tall stories from another age.

I stood and listened to a blackpowder shoot in some foothills with grass and scattered pines and a nice guy asked me if I'd like to try his Sharps. It was big and heavy and the stock had no figured wood. It smelled of gun oil and burned powder, and when I got it into firing position with the big hammer back, there was a moment when I seemed to see a little band of buffalo on a rise more than a quarter-mile away. But the buffalo had not been there for more than a hundred years and the real target was just a big gong that would ring when you hit it. More than a quarter-mile away.

Chapter Eighteen

Masters of the Hunt

The mountain-sheep hunter is a watcher and MacDougall watched well. He would not show himself or his client on open ridge-tops, for the mountain sheep is a watcher too, a resident of high places with vast open spaces before him.

MacDougall handled the instruments of his profession with care—the well-protected spotting scope, its assortment of eyepieces, and its stubby tripod firmly lashed against his packboard along with lunch necessities and a piece of rope. But whether he was on foot or horseback, the scope was always quickly available. Now, lying flat on his belt buckle, he set the tripod feet firmly in some loose gravel beside a ridgetop boulder, moving a few small stones with his hand to be sure it was solid. I watched the procedure as I had watched it many times before and breathed deep at the thin air.

I studied my rifle, which was really heavier than need be. A good stockmaker, I thought, could get some weight from the fore-end, but the barrel was too heavy and any change there would be very expensive. I was getting old for this business. I sat slumped a little and considered lying down but knew getting up again would be an effort.

MacDougall was completely still except for an occasional tiny movement of the scope as he studied ridge after ridge in a distance that became blue to the west. There were snowy peaks, enormous valleys, and endless ridges that made up most of British Columbia toward the Pacific. I stared at MacDougall—big creased hat shielding his face and scope, checkered wool shirt and Indian moccasins, the utility kind that extended up the calf and are held by thongs around the leg. He wore modern moccasin rubbers over the soft leather, low rubbers that from the top look like the kind made to go over dress shoes but have rock-grabbing cleats on the soles. I had short mountain-hunting boots with Vibram soles and MacDougall had commented that they were a lot better than what he and his fellow guides wore. So I had asked him why he wore moccasins.

"I don't know," MacDougall said. He never talked much.

After twenty minutes or so, MacDougall slipped gently back from the spotting scope, broke off a blade of grass, chewed it a little, and looked at the ground. His mind was working on Stone sheep trophy mathematics. He sat up and blinked.

"There's a fair ram couple of ridges over," he said. "One horn'll go about thirty-six inches and the other one is broomed off about an inch. He's pretty and has a lot of white on him but I'm pretty sure we can do better."

It was a typical spotting scope report, an almost supernatural estimate of horn dimensions, but I had learned it was an essential part of the game for a man who steered hunters after world records. MacDougall paused and then looked straight at me.

"There's something else," he said. "It's to hell and gone off there in the mirage—miles. It's a big, black ram and I can barely make him out, but he's got a heavy head. The whole damn sheep is big—and black. Here, take a look."

It took a little while for me to get into position for the high-powered eyepiece, and at first glance I almost gave up. I seemed to be looking into the next world—or one we had already passed. There was the wildly shimmering mirage of distance and foreshortened high ridges, nearly as high as the one we were on. When I found the spot carefully described by MacDougall, there was only one sheep—I supposed it was a sheep—showing black and with none of the mottled design generally going with Stones. My eyes smarted. I guess I saw the head as a shapeless blob. I pulled back and gawked off into space over the scope.

"Here," said MacDougall. "I'll show you the little one."

He tipped the scope a little, made a minor adjustment and let me look again. The other Stone ram was there as if flashed on a screen, posed on a grassy plot just below a boulder and above a sheet of slide rock. He had the grace of wild sheep and a perfect sweep of horns except for the tiny broomed spot on one tip, and as I watched he turned his head and seemed to stare right at me as if he could look through the scope backward. I nervously glanced around but I was sure he hadn't seen me, for my nondescript hat must have appeared as just another lump of stone on a ridge-top. I hoped that anyway.

No matter. I was caught in the trophy fever that had grown with endless spotting reports and association with hunters and guides who could recite record-book figures glibly. I hadn't intended that. I had just wanted to shoot a Stone ram and I wondered how I could have become a haggard, itchy-bearded trophy chaser in ten days.

"We can ride the horses several hours in the dark tomorrow morning," MacDougall said. "We'll leave them part way up in the buckbrush and hike up the rest of the way while it's still early."

It never occurred to him that I might not approve of that crawling, stumbling endurance event.

Back at camp, when MacDougall first examined the head carefully, he pointed at the heavy, close-curled horns, unusual for a Stone. "That's what fooled me," he said. "I wasn't sure what we had. I just knew it was big."

It was a long speech for MacDougall, and I recalled the mirage dancing between me and the indistinct sheep image in the scope. I'd just known *something* was there.

The ram really was big and black and for years appeared in the Boone & Crockett record book. I suppose it's been eliminated by now.

The master-hunter's eyes have learned their game and an examination by an optometrist will probably find nothing unusual. My father, for example, needed reading glasses early. He was never a sport hunter, and where game was concerned he had the approach of a man who sought it to eat. He could *see* cottontail rabbits. He saw them in green grass, or in dry, frosted weeds as winter came on. No matter how ornate the rabbit's form or "squat," or whatever the naturalists will call it, my father *saw* the rabbit.

I sought rabbits as a sort of holy quest, pursuing them with a variety of single-shot .22 rifles and various single-shot shotguns, but I seldom saw them if they were hiding unless there was snow. If my father became frustrated, he would show them to me. Kansas farm kids in those days were likely to use guns at an early age, long before they learned to drive a Model T Ford.

My father's rifle was a Model 90 Winchester, similar to those that served a thousand shooting galleries with .22 shorts. His had an octagon barrel and was kept taken down in a canvas and leather case. Some authorities have said it was the first really successful pump rifle.

My father used it with deliberation—or let me use it after he had pointed out the rabbit. I have stood in embarrassment and frustration while he patiently showed me where the rabbit was. Or, if I could not see it I would tell him in misery to go ahead and shoot it, and I think he often did so regretfully, fearing there was something seriously wrong with his son's eyes.

"It's right there below that little bunch of weeds by the rock. You can see his eye and his ears right above that dandelion. That shiny speck is his eye. Just shoot at that."

But if I insisted, with embarrassment, he would take out his eyeglasses from his pocket in the front of his bib overalls, put them on carefully, and shoot the rabbit with surgical precision. It would roll out of its form and he would put away his glasses. He needn't have worried as I know he did. It was years later that the U.S. Navy found nothing wrong with my eyes. My father knew what a cottontail rabbit looked like in the weeds. I didn't.

Long after cottontails, I wanted to shoot a moose and never had. I never seemed to meet any really big ones, even the ones that chased packhorses and grunted around tents. When I finally saw one I wanted, he was on the other side of a deep, fast river. I nestled the crosshairs back of his shoulder and said "bang" to myself. No way to get to him.

"Sit down and get ready and I'll call him across to our side," the guide said.

I sat down and snugged into the sling. The guide grunted and the rutting bull grunted back and started across the river. He waded deep and half swam with the current swirling around his withers. The guide grunted again and the bull brought his long front legs up on our bank. He nearly filled the scope and I groped with the crosshairs to find the right spot.

"Shoot him now," said the guide, master hunter for moose.

Chapter Nineteen

SOME

SIDELIGHTS

I t is a corny thought, but if all the upland game birds in the world were enclosed in a huge fenced-in pasture, cropped like a football field, free admission, I'd probably either sell my shotgun or go shoot nothing but clay targets.

Game birds live in wonderful places, places I wouldn't see otherwise, and those places make up most of the part I remember. Bird dogs have been my guides.

I am no world traveler, but the places I have hunted are forever marked in memory by nature and human history—often melancholy history of long forgotten people I feel I have known. The feelings are stronger when I go back another time, sometimes to find the places have been changed, landmarks erased by human progress.

• • •

It has been more than thirty-five years since I first saw the old combine sitting on grassland at the edge of wheatfields out West. Apparently it had been retired although in pretty good condition then, and someone had built a neat board fence around it to protect it from snoopy range cattle, who are prone to forcefully rub away insistent itches. Perhaps the rancher who left it planned to repair it someday—or he just couldn't deliberately junk what had been a faithful worker.

In those nearly four decades, it has rusted heavily and part of the board fence has rotted. No one will ever rebuild it and I wonder about whomever left it there and where they are today. Then, with a sort of mental jolt, I realize the old combine had been there no telling how long when I first saw it. The sharp-tailed grouse are hard for the dogs to pin in the nearby stubble each fall, leaving with monotonal *cuk-cuks* while still out of range most of the time.

• • •

Along a Montana creek the sage hens were a little scattered, exactly where the old cowboy had told us they would be, and wide-eyed dogs brought in two of the great birds, sure that we had found something big enough for celebration. Reloading with cocky satisfaction, I noticed the old cowboy who had brought us there was standing by a pile of rubble, half-hidden by sage.

"I pretty near lived on sage hens," he said. "That's my old camp shack."

• • •

Generations of pointers and gunners had shot bobwhite quail at the row of camphor trees before we went there with careful instructions. In Florida, they were not native trees, of course, but the house they stood by was long gone with only skimpy foundation lines remaining, and an old shed had lasted only a little longer. In good years there were more than one covey, and it was forty years ago when I first saw a pointer rock-solid there, but the birds had a tendency to buzz off over the underbrush along the tree line. It was easier if they turned out over the patch of partridge pea, heading down toward the oaks and the marshy spot. The first gun I used there was a pump with a pretty stock, but it had a primitive choke device and sprayed shot like a hose.

There is a beautiful brick home with a swimming pool where the quail used to be, and I guess the area has been "improved." But a couple of years ago it was incorporated into a nearby town and you couldn't shoot there now, anyway. I hope there are bird feeders for descendants of the old coveys.

• • •

I no longer feel that I am the "first" gunner anywhere. Clinging to a steep slope on Donnelly's Dome in Alaska and swinging wildly at a plunging ptarmigan in a screaming sixty-mile-an-hour gale, I noticed something at my feet that didn't fit the pattern of gravel—ancient brass heads from paper shotshells of no telling when. I saw them just as I was beginning to feel like a pioneer adventurer.

In one place, the blue grouse live far back in the Rockies, a place where you leave the truck by a skimpy, climbing two-track and take to a ridge where the only sound is the breeze in the pines until a little gust of it carries you a hint of a chainsaw working miles away. Here, I felt, no one had hunted for a hundred years—but it wasn't quite true. There is a little creek and a perfect camping spot.

"Look here," said my friend, digging in a tree hollow.

And there were crumbling lined-paper records of a hunting party that had been there repeatedly in the 1920s. The log ended in '26 as I remember, but it was a long time ago when I saw it.

"What made you dig into a hollow tree?" I wondered.

"How should I know?" said the fellow with the shotgun over his arm. "I'm going to put all this stuff back in there. Let's get the dog headed off to the left."

• • •

In Alberta there are the abandoned homesteaders' houses that hold together well in dry air, their builders long gone in a land where grainfields are enormous and occupied homes stand far apart. Many of them have had their resident coveys of Hungarian partridge, birds believed to have gotten a good foothold in Canada before they settled firmly in the United States. I am wide-eyed at these monuments to faded dreams or starting places of agricultural empires. When I have inspected one I have felt like an intruder, and when I first visited them there had been hardly any vandals.

I am not a habitual thief, but in back of one gray-weathered house I found several brown and white crockery jugs—the same as those we used to carry water to the field when I was a kid in Kansas. I thought of my wife back home and how she treasures such things. Red and I were traveling in a tight-packed little van camper together with a Brittany, bunks, galley, guns, an ice chest of sharp-tailed grouse, and more ammunition than we could possibly use. I wedged the jugs in somehow and Red was tolerant.

But before we started home I found a shining white-tailed deer skull with beautiful antlers. I stood on a rosebush slope and admired it. My wife Debie would *really* love that so I put it into the little camper and realized the jugs would have to go. We came back by the old ranch house but I didn't put the jugs back where they had been. They were real treasures, I thought, so I lined them up in the grass beside the road so someone would find them.

It was another year when Debie and I went there to hunt sharptails and Huns and we came to the same part of the country, even to passing the same old homestead. I told her how I had been forced to leave the jugs behind and had simply set them by the road for someone who would appreciate a nostalgic keepsake from another time.

"I guess I'll get them after all," Debie said. "I see they're still sitting there."

It is a lonely country, better than crowded places.

• • •

A rancher had told me where the blind was when I went there to hunt ruffed grouse in a nearby canyon that contained golden aspen, a little creek, thick brush, and bear sign. There were always mule deer and occasionally elk. But the stone blind was on a rocky ridge with rather sparse grass, not far from mountain sheep. It was built of heavy rocks to hide a single hunter and it appears as permanent as man could build it.

To get to the blind takes a little climbing, but I can often find an excuse to go there. I tell of the huns my dog once found near it years ago (actually, I think they were moving and I've never found them since) or I tell my hunting friends they should see it, even if they're tired. Once I showed it to Leighton Baker, author and modern buckskinner, muzzleloader and all.

"Doesn't look Indian to me," Leighton said. "Looks like some white man was set to bushwhack something or some-*body*."

I showed it to an archeologist. Could it be an ambush for sheep, elk, deer, or birds? I waited expectantly and the archeologist checked it again and then looked down at the town in the valley only a few miles away and up at a jetliner's white contrail against a blue highcountry sky.

"Mister," he said, "for all you know he might have been waiting for a dinosaur."

• • •

One abandoned mountain home was startling. A stranger to that country, I found a big house that was almost ornate, far up a canyon road on an expanse of nearly level ground. There was a patch of hay. There were cutthroat trout in the brushy stream that went by it and a cock pheasant cackled from there. The old pointer stopped on a steep nearby slope and for once I was ready when the ruff dived from it and leveled off, the light 12-gauge echoing more than I had expected.

I wondered how the folks from the big house got in and out during a Rocky Mountain winter. On up the canyon the wagon road faded to a skimpy outline of two tracks, and the white pointer working the aspens on the brushy slopes seemed out of place where the browns and grays of wild game would fit better. We came to a clearing, almost completely overgrown, and there were the telltale nails and scraps of glass, even a little outline of foundation. Someone had built there long before the big house came.

Then we went farther and a pair of ruffs slipped away from the dog's point and I waved my gun around foolishly, never getting a shot at all. It was a little later that we came to what was left of a rough-cut log cabin, just vine-covered scraps. The builders of the big house hadn't been the pioneers at all. Back in town all of the old-timers knew about the big house. They looked blank when I mentioned the log remnants far up the canyon.

• • •

Of all the wild residents you might meet following a bird dog, none is more furtive than the cougar, and many a lion hunter has never seen one unless it was in a trap or treed by hounds. There was once in Florida when I saw one perched on an abandoned cistern like an enlarged housecat, and once I saw a shadow that moved, grunted, and left tracks. Bird dogs don't know about such scents and may look at you inquiringly.

There are veterans of the wild country who have never heard a cougar, but I think I did. The Brittany was working grouse scent in the Rockies when both he and I stopped suddenly. From a promontory of tumbled boulders we heard what sounded like teenagers laughing and shouting—but there were no words, just the overall impression. This was no woman's scream as some naturalists describe.

"I never heard one," the cougar trapper told me, "but I know they make freakish noises. I think you heard a cat."

I killed two grouse near the rock precipice. Oh, yes, something else. A golden eagle kept circling the spot where the sounds came from. I needed an excuse to tell this and two ruffed grouse, gray phase, should entitle me to report my cat.

The big Brittany worked the edge of a steep little brushy knoll somewhere in Idaho and a coyote appeared only a few feet above him. Coyotes chase and kill dogs, and coyotes are chased and killed by dogs, but the little wolf and the Brittany faced each other for a moment and both turned away, pretending not to have noticed anything unusual. There was no code for such situations.

• • •

In Honduras we went to the dove field across great geometric designs in the land and I asked a guide about them.

"Oh, something the Mayans made at some time or other," he said. "They've been all over here."

And it was in Honduras I stood in a dove field with a warm over-under and watched an ox-cart wind slowly up a narrow road toward the top of a little volcano that smoked steadily.

I suppose I could have seen all of these things without a shotgun but I probably wouldn't have.

Chapter Twenty

COMPLETE DOVE
COVERAGE

When I started out on mourning doves a long time ago I shot pretty well with my back to a high hedge some of them were scooting over. They'd zip over my head, maybe twenty feet up, and as they left, going almost straightaway, I'd poke at them and they'd come down.

I had come from a part of the country where they didn't shoot many doves, saying they were birds of peace and really songbirds instead of game birds, so when I started whacking the ones that came over that hedge I felt a little guilty. I didn't see any with olive branches, but I didn't know that doves had been made illegal in a lot of states because nobody there could hit them. It seemed easy to me for a while and I decided my gun must be the perfect one for them. It was a Remington Model 870 pumpgun and I had gotten it second-hand. It had a custom stock with decent wood and the first owner said he'd had it designed for dove shooting.

After I showed the local boys at that hedge, we went over to a pond where they said the doves would start coming in for water toward evening. They put me in a perfect position so the birds would drop right in opposite me across a little neck of the lake, which is what they did. It was going to be a little too easy, I thought, but I figured I'd just shoot a couple more and not make a hog of myself. They hovered and I shot right at them, after which they would fly away to some other waterhole where it wasn't so noisy. I would have sneaked home, but two of the guys had ridden with me and I couldn't leave them and their doves out there with darkness coming on.

They told me I was not getting my head down properly, that I was shooting too fast and too slow, that I did not have the right choke, that my gun did not fit me, that I was aiming instead of pointing, that the shells were too hot and I was probably flinching, that I was flock shooting instead of picking out one bird and staying with it. They said I would probably get those little things straightened out the following day, but I did not go the following day. Everyone seemed to have forgotten those doves I popped coming over that hedge.

I took the nifty pumpgun with the experimental choke device and checked the pattern. No discredit to the Remington folks, who didn't make it, but the experimental choke device produced a doughnut image. At thirty yards, there was a circle of pellets with a gap inside it you could throw a banjo through. That explained why I couldn't hit the doves hovering in front of me, but I wasn't happy about the ones I had hit zooming over the hedge. By pointing off to one side, or up or down, I had knocked the stuffing out of them. Such little problems are common among dove shooters.

I got another shotgun with a choke that seemed to be right, but I guess it wasn't really a dove gun because I couldn't hit them very well, so I studied everything I could read about doves. The consensus was that doves are different, that they are careless flyers with uncertain routes, but that we couldn't kill all of them anyway because any time two doves settle on the same branch they begin to discuss starting a family, which often happens several times a year.

I went quail hunting several times with a deadeye who could give instructions to his dogs, complain that the old days were gone, and shoot quail, all at the same time. I remember his missing one bobwhite when I thought he was going to break his engraved super-light 20-gauge autoloader over the jeep bumper. I was anxious to see him collect doves, so I welcomed the chance to go to a dove field with him. I cautioned him about the legal limit and he nodded grimly.

When the doves started flying, I spent most of my time watching the deadeye, but I was far enough away I couldn't tell just how he was doing. Desert Storm must have sounded about the way he did. Finally, he stumbled over a pile of empty shells, said he was out of ammunition, and told me he never could hit doves. He said doves don't know how to fly and logical folks can't bag them. He said it's different with quail. They know where they are going. He had two birds but said he thought one of them might have been hit by a lady on the other side of the field.

I checked a dove flying alongside a country road and he was traveling thirty-seven miles an hour, apparently running scared. I had assumed they went at least seventy, but I reasoned that would be impossible for a bird flying with only one wing at a time. Of course it's different when a dove has a tailwind. I used to think they would then break the sound barrier, but I later reasoned those booms were probably caused by other shooters. A dove does not indicate what route he plans, and when over a dove field he sometimes makes right-angled turns without sticking out a wing. I have always felt they are addicted to snap decisions and may drop for fifteen or twenty feet while contemplating the next move.

After a few years of shooting at doves with several guns that seemed to hit other kinds of birds fairly well, I decided to go where a couple of hundred doves wouldn't alter the census much if I happened to get hot. I went South.

I went to Central and South America rather furtively, hoping no one would recognize me and that I would become a master dove gunner after firing a few thousand shells. At first, no one noticed me, but I eventually became pretty well known in Honduras and Colombia. I think I attracted attention because my pickup boys kept laughing. I reached a low point when a smart-aleck pickup boy yanked my nifty over-under away from me to show me how to kill birds. I did not understand his instructions in Spanish, but after he gave the gun back to me he took personal credit for every bird I got.

Most important, I got acquainted with some real dove shooters, some of whom make a year-around hobby of it the way others shoot trap or skeet. On a trip to Colombia I rode on the Trek International bus with a quiet character whose hobby is dove shooting, and to make conversation I bragged to him that I had shot 50 percent that day since I was in a perfect spot where the birds were just coasting. I told him I had bagged seventy birds and he said that was great. Then I asked him how he had done and he said it was his full-choke day and that he had made only long shots, but mumbled that he had killed 388. This "full-choke day" business bothered me because I always tried to use the choke that best fitted on a particular spot. In that case, it amounts to letting them go if I need full choke as I can't shoot that well. The next day I was on the stand next to his, an error in self-esteem.

I had a single pickup boy, who kept yawning when he wasn't laughing. The man next door was having an "improved-cylinder" day, which meant he shot only at birds within something like thirty-five yards. He used three pickup boys and they did a lot of yelling and sweating. I noticed that his pickup boys looked somewhat alike, all of them rangy and seemingly a little more mature than most of the crew. He killed a lot of birds and the next day he was back to full choke. I was deliberately next to him that time and the boys had to run a lot farther. I estimated some of the kills were around sixty to sixty-five yards and he was trying to get two thousand birds for his trip—no crime since the Colombian doves are so destructive to agriculture they are poisoned if the shooters can't control them. As one of the pickup boys ran past my stand, I think he was cursing in Spanish under his heavy breathing, but I couldn't be sure.

The true dove shooter told me about his equipment, after I asked respectfully with my hunting cap in hand. At that time it was illegal to take more than one hunting gun into Colombia and he was using a 12-gauge Beretta autoloader with two extra barrels and a neatly arranged stock of parts in a special kit. The shooter said the Beretta was quite reliable and very simple to repair if anything did go wrong. Obviously, he could fix a breakdown in the field while his pickup boys were catching their breath. He didn't downgrade any make of gun.

I believe it is to the credit of the dove that after all these years I generally cannot find one over a gun barrel. However, I have gathered a lot of instruction from real dove shooters and have broken it into easily understood rules that more adept shooters may be able to use. The most important are:

- If you are killing more than a third of the doves you shoot at, don't listen to anybody. They'll just screw you up.

- People in white tee shirts often stand in the center of open dove fields and kill birds, but probably not as many as those along the edges. They say a laughing dove does not fly steadily.

- Since it's often possible to see doves coming for a considerable distance there's a temptation to track them with the barrel long before you shoot — but it is unnecessary to kill a dove more than once, and the longer you point at him the more ways you figure to miss him.

- Pay attention to the wind, they say. It may be different up where some of the birds are, and thirty miles an hour of wind speed added to thirty miles an hour of dove speed can easily be figured with a pencil and paper. I had always felt that all doves fly with strong tailwinds but am told this is not true.

You are lucky to have all of this hot dope from a studious type like me. However, a careful survey of ammunition costs will show that chicken or turkey is much less expensive than mourning dove.

Chapter Twenty-One

SNIPE SENTIMENT

I have stood in grassy mud shifting my grip on a shotgun that has become heavy, tried to focus watering eyes on distant specks, and grown sentimental over snipe. Generally alone. My kind of snipe shooting is not social.

I have never worn a necktie to hunt snipe, and things written about them are informational rather than emotional—or writers try to be clever, of which I am guilty.

Like this:

- Don't look for empty shells to learn if your snipe have been shot up—look for empty boxes. Snipe shooters miss a lot.

- Remington shells are best to use on snipe because the boxes are green and littering hunters can build snipe habitat in the grass.

- Snipe are small and would be more popular if they were called "bog pheasants" or "mud turkeys."

- The mud on a snipe marsh is not really that deep. It's all the shells you're carrying.

- Snipe don't really yell, "Scaipe!" as they flush. Students of the subject know it's "Escape!"

- Snipe appear to fly with one wing at a time but actually just aren't paying attention.

- Snipe flocks break up frequently because they can't agree on a course.

- When a snipe dives from a great height he really considers piercing the earth's crust, but always changes his mind at the last instant and looks surprised that he was able to stop.

- When a snipe flies with ducks he just hasn't noticed he's with strangers.

- A snipe is a woodcock from the wrong side of the tracks.

Things like that.

With those matters out of the way, we have to explain that there really are snipe, even though they won't show up for scared kids left in a dark forest with burlap sacks.

I have shot at more snipe in Florida than anywhere else, but I have watched their flight-student maneuvers from a goose blind in British Columbia. I have stood deep in a western trout stream and heard their eerie mating sounds high overhead—some days later to find a mother snipe complaining shrilly of my trespass on her nesting zone. Are woodcock sounds more cultured?

There are a variety of ways to shoot snipe, but perhaps the most popular finds a group of sports descending upon a marshy pond where birds have concentrated a long way from larger marshes. I have been there: the snipe swarm up in confused groups, reluctant to leave, while shotguns pop wildly and shooters yell curses or bellow in triumph. It is not easy but such birds are naive and it is a little crude. Would anyone treat woodcock that way?

And there are learned statements about equipment for snipe shooting. Use a light, fast upland gun, open bored, for short-range speed. The small bores, I read, are excellent for such operations.

There are times and places where this advice is sound, and I recall when I used to hunt a broad marsh with thick patches of switch grass. I carried a 20-gauge double that weighed a little over five pounds and that seemed to jump simultaneously with birds that came up close to my feet, having been surprised behind grass clumps. In fact, my best snipe scores were made there, and I dote on places where there are cattail patches or clumps of maidencane with wet snipe lawns in between. But most of my snipe prefer open spaces where they can stand in short grass and a film of water, waiting for the exact moment when I am stepping through a boggy spot or looking in the wrong direction. They do not always speak when they leave, sometimes sliding away like experimental owls.

After someone built a super highway across that beautiful swamp with the switch grass, I found my snipe operations invariably took place on the open short-grass flats, and after some rather grim results I regretfully pushed the little 20 into the back of the cabinet. I did my version of scientific measurement, concluded the average snipe was thirty yards or more away before I could shoot, and started poking with a 12-gauge over-under. A modified barrel was best for me and I would have gone to full choke except that I can't point that well. I finally settled on No. 8½ shot in a skeet load.

Although the advice to walk downwind is very practical from a shooting standpoint, I have never figured how to walk back to the boat or truck without going upwind.

There is no warning, no conspiratorial dog pointing out the game, and all flushing snipe are a surprise except on those rare occasions when I see one standing upright for a better look at me. As I approach such a victim I try to keep my left foot forward, and I ignore other birds flushing nearer to me. I have very rarely killed a bird I have seen before it flushes. Surprise is better than nervous prostration.

Most snipe country, of course, demands boots, generally hip boots, and I think those lightweight gloves the clay target shooters love are a help because half an hour of walking up snipe leaves me with sweaty hands, in addition to a stiff neck and a limp caused by walking with my left foot forward.

There are rules. Focus your eyes at the distance where you expect the birds to appear and eye only a reasonable segment of the terrain. If you try to see 360 degrees of snipe you will probably spend most of the day in jerky stabs at birds that are too far away while others blast off from twelve feet—well a little more than *that*. After a few hours of this, a flushing cheep becomes a banshee scream.

A shorebird with long, narrow wings is obviously unable to take off at high speed, but the bumblebee is scientifically unable to fly. A snipe leaves pretty fast if he wants to and does not always announce his departure. I have read some British instruction stating a gunner should wait until the snipe has stopped darting and settles down before shooting. I tried that, but in many cases I was no longer able to see the snipe. This violent darting from left to right as he leaves makes a crossing shot much easier than the straightaway. I drool for the times (rare with really wild birds) when one swings back for a laughing inspection of me, making an easy high passing-shot. However, when this happens I am usually so ecstatic I miss with both barrels.

I check the same places every year, driving the little johnboat up into the shoreline weeds on the lake's edge, and when the twenty-five-horse motor quits I may pole a little farther before I wade to the scene of operations.

If there are snipe where I hope for them I congratulate myself on my knowledge of habitat, and when there are none I wonder why they have chosen another spot that looks the same to me.

My hunt over, I do not approach the little backcountry landing with enthusiasm, for too often there will be people there—casual fishermen, or, worst of all, those vicarious anglers who appear at boat ramps in street clothes to inquire how everyone did fishing. The fact that I am wearing a hunting vest and taking a cased shotgun from the boat does not deter those who seek stirring tales of angling prowess. It is a very poor fishing lake anyway.

"How's fishing?"

Now the simplest way out of this, if duck season is open, is to say I was hunting ducks instead of fishing, and that I found none at all. But when duck season is closed I wince and say I have been hunting snipe. The response will be dramatic. There is the officious interrogator who will become immediately incensed because he is a worldly soul who knows there is no such thing as snipe (maybe I should say I have been shooting unicorns). There is the naturalist who wants to know what they look like and I tell him they are smaller than geese. There is the real snooper who demands to see what I have killed and voices surprise that they are nothing but "little birds."

There are things about snipe I do not discuss at the ramp. I do not tell them of tiny birds with slender wings that nest in the Arctic or a little farther south, that make long migrations, some of them over great expanses of ocean, and arrive at their wintering grounds after escaping frustrated gunners for thousands of miles. I do not tell them that these are the only true shorebirds able to support open seasons, long after others became too scarce, and that a snipe can fly with a flock of blue-winged teal.

I do not mention that true snipe shooters have been around since the Civil War and that one wealthy addict of more than a hundred years ago shot many thousands of them in Louisiana with servants to pick them up. I don't speak of the times when there are effective snipe decoys on bare mud flats, even today.

The fact is I don't like to talk about snipe shooting to just anybody.

Upland Sprinters

The world's most famous pointing dogs do their work on bobwhite quail, woodcock, or ruffed grouse. The basic scene presents a high-tailed pointer or setter, frozen in picturesque style, with the concealed birds two or three steps ahead.

After the handler has carefully adjusted the statue's tail a degree or two nearer to twelve o'clock, somebody is supposed to step past and watch the birds take off. In some of the higher class quail cover somebody calls out, "Mark!" although this announcement, what with all the excitement, is generally unheard.

After the shooting, the dog stands there with the superior look only a successful pointing dog can achieve and continues to pose until someone suggests he stop pointing and find more birds. Dogs that deal mainly with "Wild West" game have a different look.

Instead of chiseled dignity, for example, a pointer of blue quail, regardless of breed, tends to have a cheerfully scheming and furtive air about him, and when he first points he seems to indicate: "This is just the beginning of the program, buster. If you pay attention we might get you a shot at some birds."

He is then likely to lift a foot gently, crouch a little, and roll his eyes toward various clumps of weeds, bushes, and cactus. The blue quail, also known as "cottontop" or "scalie," is the standard bearer for those western birds that use their wings strictly as a last resort. Some blue-quail hunters do not use dogs, and although these people invariably operate in the West and likely have large hats, they do not wear high-heeled boots. They tend to be a little on the lean side, have earned high school track letters, and specialize in running very fast with various types of shotguns in hand.

It is accepted that sound is likely to make blue quail fly instead of run, and if you must yell while chasing them, it is good for morale to have something appropriate to say. It is the same sort of situation that has gained reputations for mule drivers, drill sergeants, and boatswain mates, and some colorful phrases have been developed by gunners while ripping through cactus after scaled quail. Some feel dogs cheat by smelling birds.

Of course, one of the better ways of shooting blue quail involves a beat-up pickup, a frustrated off-road auto racer, and a shooter whose track letter is not too out of date. When the quail cross the dusty two-track, they appear as white-topped legless little objects riding atop small blurs, which are actually their legs beginning to wind up.

As the birds are sighted, the man riding shotgun yells, "There go the little bastards!" after which he dismounts in a lunge, trying not to catch his 12-gauge crosswise in the door. He gives chase to the quail while the driver crashes the pickup into a sage bush and follows at top speed on foot. If the quail have time, they will scatter and disappear—generally. However, scalies are masters of improvisation and the situation remains fluid. There have been a great many books written about bobwhite quail, ruffed grouse, and wood-cock. I have not seen a book on blue quail although I am certain someone is working on one and has thrown away several drafts.

Although the running-bird line is generally accepted as going north and south through Kansas, with mannerly game to the east and rude game to the west, pheasants have done the running thing in the East for many years.

The Gambel's quail and the California, or valley quail, are noted as sprinters, and it is confusing to learn that they inter-breed. I do not know what the cross should be called or what it looks like but suspect it comes with little track shoes.

I was disturbed by a western movie in which mounted travelers are crossing a desert and one of them says they are nearing water because he sees a Gambel's quail. At this point we are shown a large white bird flapping past, looking a great deal like a white heron, and I wonder if *that* is the result of cross-breeding California quail and Gambel's.

During a foray into Mexico, I viewed the running Gambel's at its best. It has been many years, and I feel the story can now be told. My companions were upland gunners of a high type and at least one of them owned a kennel of blue-ribbon pointers. I do not think he had heard the terms "ground-sluicing" or "pot-shooting." He would expect a tiger to fly.

The guide did not have a dog, and although he spoke English he did not scatter it around unnecessarily. The hunting area was a network of deep-dusted passageways winding among incredible walls of briers. The dust was solidly patterned with quail tracks except where a big snake had traveled recently. Soft quail hoots were almost constant. A squad of birds scooted across a passageway and into another tangle. One of the hunters rushed to the brush where the birds had disappeared and kicked it violently but nothing happened.

"Quails do not fly," the guide explained. "Shoot on ground."

We pretended not to hear the ground business and kept trying to kick up a bird. We got separated and once I saw a quail fly for about twenty feet but couldn't get on him in time. Some time later, I put up a bird that left on the other side of some brush and I banged away through the thorns and scored. I do not know what kind of a bird it was but I found it was not a quail.

When we gathered at the truck I had no birds at all. The man with all the bird dogs back home had two quail. He said it was hard to learn to shoot running birds, but he was catching on to it. He then told just what sort of custom shotgun would be ideal for ground-sluicing running Gambel's through the brush. We decided not to report what had happened, but I think the statute of limitations has run out.

The chukar, an immigrant from the dry mountains of Europe and Asia, is not only a runner but insists on doing it uphill. When annoyed by clawing hunters or befuddled pointing dogs, a chukar starts sprinting upward and generally does not fly until he runs out of mountain. To make them behave for a dog they must be approached from above. I have bagged my last mountain chukar, and I sat down for a long while afterward, regretfully concluding that my chukar years had passed.

Unbeknownst to casual guests who haven't watched them much, the big western sage grouse is quite a hiker, and I have known them to move roughly a mile ahead of a careful dog before taking off. My best sage-hen story concerns the time my dog worked for a long way and then pointed where a narrow, deep wash came down the hillside. The ditch was very narrow at the bottom and no more than five or six feet wide at the top. I looked in and found the birds bunched together several feet down and staring straight up at me. No room to fly. (I have hesitated to tell this on the poor old sage hens that take off slowly at best and have had bad press concerning their intelligence.) Sage hens don't usually hide in ditches. These birds just got in there and didn't figure how to get out.

The good Hun dog is a shifty, grinning character who looks back for his hunter every time he sniffs birds and is impatient if you are too slow. A real canine martinet has been known to purposely jump birds when his hunting party dawdles. I have attempted open-country Huns with a cultured English pointer who felt a picture point was sacred, and for all I know his trainer had worn polished boots. He cruised the country-side in high gear and ignored our plodding progress behind him. I whistled at him once and he sneered.

The pointer had a regal air and when it was time to point he froze like the cover picture on a dog-training manual. The first time this happened I stood in awe for a long moment and then walked up side by side with my friend, who automatically took the opposite flank of the pointer. We passed the dog, kicked a couple of bushes, and continued on as if approaching an enemy trench system. We went over a little rise and down into a considerable draw with a creek at the bottom, at which point I missed my dog and wondered how he had lost the route. I then retraced my steps and saw the porcelain pointer still frozen. Having forgotten what the man had told me to do when I wanted to "break" a point (a new problem for me), I knelt before the dog and explained to him that the Huns had left, if indeed he'd had some in the first place. The dog did not blink.

Then I recalled that a tap on the head meant it was time to start over, and he began hunting again. Late that day we flushed the birds wild when we came back almost a quarter of a mile from the pointing site, across a near-canyon and a considerable creek.

We hear a lot about birds that run too much, even ruffed grouse and bobwhites, and my peasant explanation is that the birds that fly get shot. I think if you'll leave a community of bobwhites alone for a few generations they will hunker down under a pointer's nose and give somebody a chance to yell, "Mark!" instead of, "What's the matter with that damned dog?"

In west Texas the setter and the pointer went birdy, slipped under a fence and cat-footed through some weeds, through a patch of sunflowers, and past several mesquite trees. When they stopped and pointed you could barely see the setter's tail and something white that had to be the other dog.

The man from Mississippi went through the tight fence like a man who had crossed a fence before and was almost to the dogs before they moved and went another thirty yards. The dogs pointed and three bobwhites went up in three directions. The man from Mississippi deftly swatted the nearest one with his 20-gauge humpbacked Browning, and his friend on the other side of a mesquite got one too. You could hear some other birds taking off but they were scattered.

"Everywhere I go these days, the birds run," said the man from Mississippi.

Chapter Twenty-Three

YEARS OF SAGE HENS

Ｗe had a dog pointing into an alfalfa field. When we went over there a bunch of big sage grouse battered their way into the air, but before they could really get going we shot a couple of them. This sounds good, but I really wasn't satisfied.

I do not like sage hens in alfalfa fields. I want sage hens out where the sage hills have no end, looking hazier in the distance, and where there is little sign of human agriculture. I can accept a distant ranch house, preferably long abandoned, and I like to see sheepherder monuments on the high ridges. But I am bothered by highways, and even an airliner's contrail breaks the scene I like to think is unchanged since the wagons first creaked westward. I want distant antelope and those wind-tattered high clouds that have always marked the West.

Sage grouse have limited range that can be limited further as diesel monsters tear the sage brush into wheatland, but they make gains here and there. They're a western bird but the distribution maps vary with their ups and downs. There are some in southern Canada.

Don't preach to me about sage grouse sporting qualities. They sometimes flush wild, and I have walked all day without a shot at an estimated thousand birds. They sometimes hold until their wings brush your vest as they leave. As they take off they fight for altitude and barely gain at first. Once they are underway they go at typical grouse speeds and are so big I shoot behind them. They sometimes lie perfectly for pointing dogs, and sometimes they pace off under the sage, perhaps for almost a mile. It is easy to believe your soft-footed, eye-rolling dog has lost his mind.

Now and then you may sight a covey hurrying over a ridge where the sagebrush pattern is broken, shadows that disappear again so that you are not quite sure what you saw. Where there have been large numbers, some hunters have studied hillside openings with binoculars before ever leaving their trucks. I don't know of any spot today where that would be a practical approach, but then I don't know all the sage hen places. I've tried, but there hasn't been time. Anyway, few hunters simply walk off into strange sage country without knowing where birds have been seen. Sometimes it takes a lot of searching, even then.

Light upland loads will not penetrate a five-pound body from the rear, and where there have been sloppy hunters our dogs have found too many cripples. At modest ranges, there are a few shooters who go for small shot and count on hitting heads and wings. I'll take heavy loads and big shot.

I have always used pointing dogs, although flushing dogs can be excellent, especially when the birds are not scattered over too wide an area. There is nearly always cactus, but usually not enough to be more than a minor hazard. Sage country can be rattlesnake country when weather is warm.

For me, the worst hazard has been pronghorns, for there are a few dogs who never learn that the dry-land racers have a playful streak when pursued by a yipping rebel. They loaf just a little ahead of him for as far as he will chase, and when they finally leave him, stagger-tired and lost, he may be miles from where he started. A short tour is enough for most dogs, but there are a few addicts who learn slowly and may not backtrail to their hunting party, at least on the same day they left.

Through the years I have learned a number of areas that have no birds at all until certain times during the fall, each area seeming to have its own dates. I know of one such series of sagebrush draws with one creek that gets a flock of about thirty birds around mid-October each year. It's about the same number every season, and we have tried not to over-shoot them. When we laid off entirely one year, there were no more than usual the next season. I suspect that if we really shot them out, the area would be ruined for a very long time.

For years I had shot sage grouse from what I thought were two flocks, generally found about two miles apart along an immense coulee. We pretty well cleaned out one bunch, but counted on the other flock to hold up. There had been only one bunch that lived in two places. Will they ever come back?

But I have hunted sage grouse where they numbered in hundreds and possibly thousands, and on several occasions I have been present when the birds had just moved in. The migrations seem to be from one sea of sage to another almost like it, and I do not know the reasons.

On one of my first sage-hen hunts, two of us were driving a two-track in the high pasture country when a bird walked across the trail ahead of us. We stopped, got out, and found we were surrounded by birds making no effort to hide. We walked a few steps, and they began to take off. So I killed my limit of three and had walked no more than ten yards. Tame birds, easy shots.

But we were on the edge of a vast concentration, and it was just as easy the next day. We hunted that place for years at the right time each fall. But when I think of standing among gawking "sage turkeys," I also recall stumbling along, a little too tired, with a frustrated dog watching sage hens flush in what seems an endless curtain of them a hundred yards away.

A widely scattered covey sometimes gets up as suicidal singles with the gunners in their midst, but this program can

go sour if a dog loses his cool when he finds himself surrounded by five-pound birds with the guns still a hundred
yards back. Let's put in here that there is nothing "classic"
about sage-hen hunting. I am fascinated by it, but some of my
grouse- and quail-shooting friends think both the sage hens
and I are a little strange.

I shoot a bird near an ancient trail, and a pointer brings it
to me, his eyes bulging to see over his giant prize. I see a
broken scrap of rusty iron almost hidden by a bunch of
prickly pear. It may have come from somebody's patched
pickup bed, but I like to think it might have been part of a
creaking prairie schooner.

Sage grouse fly through history.

Chapter Twenty-Four

GHOSTS AND GUNPOWDER

Thee were some old shotgun loading tools lying around the farmhouse where I grew up and there were a few metal cases with them, but they didn't mean much to me. Certainly they could not compare with the Civil War musket I sawed off to make a more convenient toy.

Concerned more with cowboys and Indians than with things like ducks or prairie chickens, I did not know the stray pup I had adopted was mostly English setter. Finally, I just threw the loading tools away or lost them, and although my mother had told me who they had belonged to I wasn't interested. Even though I had decided to be an outdoor writer (I didn't know the term) at the age of seven, my more immediate interests focused on cowboys and Indians. Shotgun users seemed pretty prosaic to a kid with Civil War grandfathers and a great uncle who had been some sort of a gunfighter in Texas. I think he was a horse thief but can't prove it. With no other survivors from his part of the family I guess I can tell it any way I want to.

I tried to pump lurid stories from two farm hands who had carried rifles to French trenches, but was disappointed in their modest accounts. It was years before I suddenly stopped whatever I was doing and realized I had known true heroes with fixed bayonets. It was more than fifty years before I wanted the old loading tools and also remembered I had once used a sleek and light muzzle-loading double built for a true upland gunner's hands. The name on it meant nothing to me and I have forgotten it.

I began shotgunning with all sorts of inexpensive tools, finally reaching what I had assumed was a pinnacle with a hammerless pumpgun. I learned to shoot a few aerial targets with a rifle but was a shotgun peasant, and "shooting flying" as a special sport came to me about two hundred years after it began elsewhere. Then, when digging up shooting history for a book now long out of print, I found that wingshooting hadn't really gone big until somewhere around 1850 and that it was after the Civil War that the "golden age" of shotgunning began to grow. But even the British traditions of driven game and the revered "game gun" didn't mean anything to me until about the 1950s. Although "gunning" comes a little stiffly to a country boy who went "hunting" instead, I have found the tradition-loving shotgunner is alive and well, however scarce.

With a reverence for inexact history common to old men, I have felt the ghosts of hunting dogs and their masters in a hundred places—abandoned shacks near cotton fields, nearly overgrown fences in ruffed grouse country, even at the edge of Cow Creek in Kansas where the bobwhite covey lived for all those years before I even thought of quail hunting with dogs. There are covers that have come and gone and revived again through man's whims of lumbering or farming. Once I stood on a Nevada mountainside to hear the soft cackling of chukars high on a rocky slope and regretted that I brought no tradition with me. Foreign bird and tourist hunter.

But there on the Nevada mountain I startled myself with a concept I had not met before. Was I a part of the beginning of

a shooting tradition, something that might last a hundred years? Was my dog, at the moment circling a boulder with the faint scent of game, preparing to leave his own ghost there with mine?

There is the old homesteader's cabin far up the rocky canyon where I have found ruffed grouse—western ruffed grouse that lack the sophistication of eastern birds and so far lack the reverence due them. In the thirty years I have passed it annually, the old cabin has settled noticeably, seeming somehow to withdraw within itself with age and weather, and now there is a loose log that had not fallen last year. Already there are the ghosts of my bird dogs there, dogs that once led me to the aspen patches on the canyon's walls—no longer ordinary dogs but special and all-knowing ghost dogs, their frailties forgotten and only their staunch points and unswerving loyalty remembered.

There is the little highcountry groove where the Hungarian partridge have been for all those years. Though seemingly like dozens of other such coulees it hides a little spring at its base—and the owner of the land is the third who has had it since I first went there. He doesn't know where the place is. It is a good place to leave the ghosts of dogs and their masters, and I am sure that the same ghosts can stay in many places.

Ghosts are in the mind of the beholder, and maybe it is the wrong term for what is simply a consciousness that someone has at some time experienced the same places and things that I have or might have. It is the same sort of thing that causes tourists, myself included, to walk through ghost towns or forgotten cemeteries, to stand on old battlefields and imagine the sounds of war. Harmless pastime indulged in by thousands or millions of people who will admit to nothing more than a little curiosity. I know better. They wouldn't walk through a World War II battleship just to note how armament has been improved. There are ranks of ghosts in such places, sharing great and terrible things.

For years I hunted quail near a small town in Florida—a town that grew and joined other towns until the traffic became the dull rumble that city dwellers become accustomed to and do not even hear. There is one spot where the dogs would point the birds on fairly open ground, almost against a swamp, and when flushed they would buzz into the thick cover while we would try frantically to shoot quickly enough at darting shadows against a mottled quail-colored background.

Developers came to that pasture and built homes, attractive enough places, and a church appeared where two generations of dogs used to begin making game. For all I know, there are still quail in the yards, but there are no ghosts any more. I haven't seen the place for several years.

Have I actually seen something besides the shadows of an earlier time of shooting? Well, there was the old fellow I shared a sort of community duck blind with when I was very young and trying to hit close-in teal bullets with my thirty-inch barreled, full-choked pumpgun, the only shotgun to be considered by any true agricultural nimrod. I never got the fellow's name but he looked as if he had been in a duck blind before (we'd reached it at the same time and he'd accepted fate). I was fascinated by his gun—a great lever-actioned Winchester, which I know now was a 10-gauge model of 1887. Even that great old pumpgun, the '97, came ten years after it. He was really from another time but I never thought of that until much later.

I knew a man who in 1946 had been a commercial fisherman in Alaska for many years. He looked like a man who had been a commercial fisherman in Alaska for many years. He used a well-worn 12-gauge Winchester pump except for geese, when he used a 10-gauge Ithaca double—and I did not realize his vast knowledge of California waterfowl until after he was gone. Long since I have felt that he watched high flocks with me and muttered that they were too far.

I remember best my mother saying to me, "Those old shotgun things belonged to_____." But I cannot recall who it was and the ghosts will not help me.

THE GREAT
OUTDOORS

Chapter Twenty-Five

ROAD BOATS

Although I am a little short on nautical terminology, I believe I have as long a background with boat trailers and cartop boats as any current author, and it would be a shame not to give the sporting world benefit of some really basic experience.

My first boat trailer was a four-wheeler and was constructed from the running gears of what was then called a top buggy. This gave me a truly fundamental foothold in trailer care and maintenance and a scorn for current manuals. The wheels were wooden with steel tires and required considerable attention. As soon as the wood got a little dried out, the rig would have sounded like a drill team equipped with castanets except that the Model T Ford I pulled it with drowned out most of the clickity-clack. The solution was to soak the wheels so that the spokes would tighten up in the rims. A newer buggy would have had tighter spokes, but newer buggies were being used for courting girls instead of hauling cedar rowboats.

The rowboat got an easier ride, believe it or not, than most modern bass boats do because it was a spring buggy—not a primitive buckboard. Besides, the boat weighed plenty, and usually traveled with an inch of water inside since I never seemed able to keep it soaked up any better than I kept the trailer spokes wet. I hauled that boat for some time and the trailer collapsed, fortunately at the edge of a lake. Eventually the old rowboat disappeared. I think someone shot it when I wasn't around.

As I recall, that was the boat I was using when the bass attacked me. It was late evening and I was paddling a creek while another kid fished. I trailed my fingers in the water while I watched him cast, and a bass whacked me across the knuckles. I wish I could say it was a ten-pounder, but it was just a little old twelve-inch largemouth. To make the story better, I tried to find a skinned place across my hand, but there was nothing but a little red streak. I know how big the fish was because I'm sure my friend caught it very shortly afterward. The bass had been chasing bait all over the pool and my fingers looked good to him.

It was some time later that I began using cartop boats, a subject of some merriment to roadside observers, who would ask me loudly if I really thought it was going to rain that much. It got kind of tiresome.

I generally carried boats and canoes bottomside up. My friend Jack Gowdy built a galvanized metal boat and carried it rightside up atop his car. He once got caught in a real toadchoker of a rain, and the boat took on so much water that Jack's tires went flat. There was no drain plug in the boat, so Jack drove a nail through the bottom and the old Buick's tires came up.

I had a series of cartop boats and canoes, long after really good trailers were available. I was somewhat handicapped in this mode of seamanship because my wife is quite small. The problem is not that small wives cannot hold up their end (usually the bow) when loading cartop boats, but that small wives look helpless to bystanders at boat launching spots. This causes all sorts of destructive chivalry. Whereas my wife and I worked out highly efficient loading procedures for each boat, it was the headlong attack by helpful bystanders that dented the car top, broke the windows, or caused the boat to pin me to the ground.

We'd have the boat perfectly balanced and I would be sliding it on the rack (I wouldn't be able to see where I was going since I'd be underneath it) and Debie would be steering it neatly. Then, suddenly, there would be a violent jerk in one direction or another as some nice fellow tried to help the small wife. I found that former football tackles were especially hard to block out of the action.

We went a little overboard on cartoppers because our trailer hitch was used to pull a travel trailer. Somebody finally built a metal marvel that would put a 300-pound aluminum boat on top of our 1951 Oldsmobile. The loading process, which involved all sorts of engineering principles dealing with stress and leverage, was so interesting and complex in itself that fishing became secondary. But our loader was kid stuff compared to that of a traveling anthropologist we met at a saltwater ramp. He dressed as if he expected to meet Dr. Livingstone at any moment and carried a very long hunting knife at all times. He and his wife towed a big travel trailer behind a truck and carried a big skiff with mounted outboard motor on top of the pulling outfit. Since it was impossible to guess how he had gotten it up there, a crowd of local people gathered to watch. I noticed experienced professional boatmen stayed at the back of the spectators.

Sure enough, a steel ramp materialized from a forest of mechanical gadgetry and the boat rolled down to the local boat hoist, the whole process taking only an hour and a half. The gallery applauded and everybody was there again when he reloaded. I didn't like the anthropologist because he told me that my cartop outfit (atop a GMC 4X4 carryall) would not work. Even when I explained that I had been using it successfully for two years, he told me again that it would not work. You will recall that scientists have proved a bumblebee can't fly.

Boat trailering has come a long way to arrive at the concrete ramps and parking lots of today. Quite a few unusual units were produced. For example, I knew a Florida doctor who owned one of the fastest boat trailers ever used. Having spent some time aground on mud banks and oyster bars along Florida's southwest coast, he felt that a combination cabin cruiser and airboat would solve the problem, so he began with an outboard cruiser and mounted an aircraft engine and propeller on the bow. Any time the outboard ran out of water he'd touch off the airplane engine.

That wasn't so remarkable, but his wife told me that they also used the airplane engine to lighten the load on the towing vehicle.

"This was my husband's idea," she said. "We could go very fast on the highway with one of us driving the car and the other running the airplane engine."

With this combination they found no way to utilize the outboard motor as well, but I understand two highway patrolmen started drawing early retirement pay after sighting them barreling down the highway north of Miami.

We've used piggyback boats quite a bit in tidal creeks or other backcountry areas for fishing or duck hunting. We started with little plywood jobs and then used aluminum prams and johnboats. When we got to a creek our sixteen-foot boat wouldn't go through because of brush, we'd anchor it and use the piggyback.

The piggyback would be ten or twelve feet long, and when it was nested in the bigger boat somebody could ride in it along with a variety of gear. When we trailered, we'd let the piggyback outfit travel much as it did on the water, the little boat securely lashed inside the bigger one, and sometimes fastened in upside down. One little boat that we hauled many times was painted a dull tan, about the same color that's commonly used on tarpaulins. This whole outfit would trailer just fine, and before the speed limit was reduced we'd slide along about sixty-five miles an hour, same as the rest of the traffic.

On one occasion I was driving at a pretty good clip when somebody pulled alongside.

"Hey!" yelled the other driver. "The tarp blew off your boat back there a piece! It went right by my windshield and over my car. Barely missed me!"

I thanked the man and pulled over, but since there had been no tarp on the boats I was a little puzzled. But not for long. The poor guy didn't know the "tarp" that had whipped over his windshield was a hundred-pound johnboat instead of a piece of canvas.

We went back up the highway and found the johnboat well off the road to one side. The rope had frayed. The boat had been upside down and the wind had gotten under it. After that, I tied piggybacks so securely I needed a Bluejacket's Manual to undo the knots.

An old fishing friend of mine believed in getting what he called a "soon start" and we often arrived at a rural boat ramp in gray dawn. We got there one chilly morning when there was a little mist fog on the water. A man was sitting there and greeted us cheerily. He watched us launch. Funny time and place for a nature watcher but we asked no questions. As we prepared to shove off, I noticed a boat that appeared to be anchored some distance from the ramp.

"By the way," the man said, "Would you be so kind as to check my boat out there and see if you can unfasten it from the trailer? You see the whole works went into the water and the boat floated with the trailer under it."

We stared at the boat which, sure enough, appeared to be slightly tilted and quite rigid.

"My car's down there too," the man added. "But I don't suppose there's anything you could do about that."

Submerged cars at boat ramps are not particularly novel, but I like a man who handles such things with class, never batting an eye.

Back to Florida, where many of my boating adventures have taken place:

It was on Highway 27 that we misplaced a sixteen-foot boat, a trailer, and sundry other equipment in addition to a dozen duck decoys. We were headed for the Everglades swamps from upstate and were wheeling along at a very late hour. It was nice to travel late at night because there wasn't much traffic. I think it was around midnight when we noticed something was amiss. We'd passed Palmdale headed south and I had just turned off 27 onto S.R. 29, headed for LaBelle, when it occurred to me that I was no longer being followed by a boat and trailer, a fact I mentioned to my wife. The rest of this story has become a part of Florida folklore, but you might have missed it.

Now when I pull a boat I check very frequently in the rear-view mirror, probably oftener than I realize. It becomes routine and it is impossible for me to tell just when I did it last. In this case I didn't know when the last check had occurred, but it seemed strange I hadn't noticed when my load suddenly became lighter.

I got out and found the trailer hitch ball had come loose, the nut having unscrewed. Evidently I hadn't fastened it properly to begin with, but I felt this was no time to study trailering procedures. We had grim visions of the freestyle boat and trailer crashing into the car of some tourist family or ending up in the grillwork of an eighteen-wheeler, so we started back northward, going slowly and staring fearfully at the moonlit roadsides.

We found no boat and no wreck. Up near Sebring we inquired at some all-night places and no one had heard of a boat and trailer running around on their own. We started south again. (I am sorry you do not have a map of this scene). With Debie driving slowly, I was standing with the right front door open and playing a big flashlight wherever a boat might hide. I saw a lot of beer cans and a couple of stray cats.

We'd gotten almost to the Fisheating Creek bridge when Debie put on the brakes and said there was a funny mark in the road. It was the kind of mark that might have been made by the end of a trailer that was in a hurry and carrying some weight. We stared about. Far out in broad and shallow Fisheating Creek (about fifty yards out there in a solid mat of floating hyacinths) was a tiny red light that wasn't too hard to identify as the dry-cell-powered taillight of our trailer. The boat was partly sunken with the trailer beneath it, the bow being submerged. Although this is not your ideal situation, I could not imagine being happier than I was upon finding my boat in Fisheating Creek.

I waded and swam to it, digging through hyacinths. I unfastened the boat from the trailer and it barely floated, so I started bailing, pushing duck decoys and other floatables out of the way. Then I floundered toward shore, leading the skiff. I went back for the trailer, which was on the bottom, of course, but I managed to lead it along pretty well down there except for some of the floating hyacinths that hung down and tangled it.

Even as I addressed the situation in frank terms, I wished I had seen that outfit leave the highway at the bridge approach and skim clear out there with the wheels down.

We worked the trailer up the bank until we could winch it to the car. Then we winched the boat up to where we could start it onto the trailer. The total loss was one trailer ball nut and a night's sleep.

I look out the window and see our modest fishing boat sitting smugly on a galvanized trailer. The whole thing was built on purpose, and the trailer hitch on the car will probably be intact, even if the car is pulled apart.

We've come a long way, but some of the challenge is gone.

Chapter Twenty-Six

BUMBOAT

There are some beautiful houseboats on the water these days. When I meet one of them, I pull my skiff over into the weeds and watch it pass in awe. If I had the right kind of flag, I'd dip it.

These houseboats are different from ours, which was a sort of prototype. Its name, which we never painted on the hull, was *Bumboat*. That's a name that has been popular for certain craft in Chinese rivers, but our boat was not in China. It lived mostly in Everglades City and the Ten Thousand Islands of southwestern Florida.

The idea for *Bumboat* was to tow a fishing boat behind it, living on it while we fished the distant bays and creeks between Everglades City and the southern tip of Florida. The idea took on a sort of reality when a company that could build it was identified. They weren't listed as houseboaters in the phone book. The first visible evidence of our houseboat was a diagram on the shop floor. A man in a carpenter's apron stood and studied it. He kept shaking his head and I think now that was an omen.

When the boat was delivered to Everglades City two months late, it was mounted on a heavy-duty trailer. The guy in the truck that had towed it left the area at high speed. As I recall, the driver had the check in his teeth, as he did not take the time to put it in his pocket.

A quickly gathered group of us walked around the boat and admired it and then wondered how we would get it into the water. There was no launch ramp, and although the old boat hoist could handle it, no one could figure out how to fasten the hoist to the boat. Fortunately, I had a four-wheel-drive truck. It was touch and go, but the truck and I narrowly managed to avoid going into the Barron River with *Bumboat*. When she decided to go over that steep bank into deep water, she didn't fool around, making quite a splash, but finally floating. After that the bystanders wandered off and Everglades City went back to normal.

I was already thinking ahead and began to wonder how to get *Bumboat* back out when the time came. The late Ted Smallwood, resort and dock operator, said he would have a yoke and lift-out rig built to get it out with the regular hoist, so I quit worrying. When Ted built something, there was little likelihood of its bending or breaking. I went up to the shop where the recovery rig was being built and asked a man with a blowtorch if it would handle the houseboat all right. He pushed up his visor.

"Mister," he said, "if Everglades City has enough electricity, this rig will lift the Battleship Missouri, providing all the sailors get off."

We powered the houseboat with a second-hand, twenty-five-horsepower outboard motor, which was considered quite a banger in that era. The motor was very reluctant and usually started on roughly the twenty-fifth pull. I never understood why the first few pulls never produced anything but muscular development, but once the engine started it scorned idling and would quit if you throttled it back. When I approached the river dock on an incoming tide, residents of the adjacent trailer park and local motel would rush out to watch. It beat anything on television.

On her shakedown cruise, we took *Bumboat* out into Chokoloskee Bay and found that because of her high silhouette, she would not turn into a six-knot wind. For nonsailors like me, this means that if you are headed south with a six-knot wind coming from the north, the only way to turn around and head back where you came from is to put the engine in reverse and back around until you are correctly aimed. I had never used this maneuver before, but learned it with surprising speed when encircled by oyster bars.

On our first trip, we took off with a party of four, towing two fishing skiffs and heading for Alligator Bay, but our trip happened to coincide with the lowest tide on record. When we reached Oyster Bay, we had to get out and push. Actually, Oyster Bay at extreme low tide is mainly a broad flat of damp oysters.

We anchored in what is shown as Tarpon Bay on the charts, which is north of Alligator Bay. That's a main boat route now, but we spent more than a week there and saw only one other boat. He was lost.

As official captain, I soon learned there were some little inconveniences. We bought a generator for electricity, but in operation it sounded like a World War II training plane and shook the boat until it was necessary to use dull forks while eating. We replaced it with a Coleman lantern, but after the power plant was shut down for good, we continued to scream at each for some time out of habit.

On one trip I was asleep in an upper bunk when the only other guy aboard stopped reading and stood up to stretch, knocking the lantern off its hook and onto the deck. I moved pretty fast. It was the only time I recall actually picking up something with my hands without touching down with my feet, but there was no fire—at least that time.

The fire happened when the boat was back at dock and we were away. We'd left a glass bottle of water on deck and the sun used it to set the rig afire. Someone put it out and the burn patch was hardly noticeable.

Marine toilets are not noted for efficiency, but the one on the houseboat, I believe, was either an experimental model or a prototype of a prototype. It did not cost very much and turned out to be worth less than that.

After considerable experience, I found it fairly easy to unstop. I'd just get overboard and stand in the mud under the catwalk that went along both sides. Generally, the water was only three or four feet deep when I had to use the ingenious tools I designed just for toilet cleaning.

Fixing the toilet was a break in routine, occurring only two or three times each twenty-four hours. It was most challenging at night when there were so many mosquitoes under the catwalk that they had to shift position together. In winter, there weren't many mosquitoes but the water was chilly. For a time I looked for the guy who designed the toilet, but I think someone else beat me to it. He may have designed the power plant too, for all I know.

Until we bought the houseboat we had no idea how many friends we had. Most of them were amazed at the vastness of the brackish Everglades swamp—for about the first eight hours. After that, they became experts. "If you're not going out fishing for a while," they'd say, "just let me take the skiff around the corner a little piece. I think I know where I am now."

If we had two skiffs alongside, I might consent. If we were using only one small boat, I would get a little cranky. It's bad enough to prowl the swamps in a boat looking for a mesmerized man with a fly rod, but wading and swimming in search of one did not appeal to me.

There was the matter of the catwalks along the sides of *Bumboat*. If you watched your diet, you could navigate along them pretty well if there was no sea running. One of the spoilsport rules I announced as soon as anyone new came aboard was that no one should try to negotiate the catwalk with both hands full—unless they could grab the guardrail with their teeth. I emphasized that this rule was especially important when there was dew or rain.

My wife was working in the little galley when she noticed a guest attempt to step into a skiff from the catwalk with both of his hands filled with fishing tackle. She was watching from either a window or a hatch, whichever is the correct houseboat term. Debie announced crisply that our guest was nearly submerged, but that his feet and lower legs were protruding from the water in an agitated state. Further investigation revealed that he had gone in from the catwalk headfirst, obviously with grace, and that the upper part of his body was submerged vertically, upside down in the mud bottom. Low tide.

I have since reasoned that he did not disappear completely because of his generally rotund silhouette, which probably accounted for his leaving the catwalk to begin with. When he reappeared, there was considerable mud in his hair and ears. This episode caused me to adopt a rule of never anchoring over shallow water where there was a rock bottom.

On one occasion I set forth from the home port alone. The steering wheel was at the front of the cockpit with the cabin ahead of that, which meant the coxswain had to peer over the cabin while underway. There was a useful foredeck ahead of the cabin where we generally stored cans of gasoline and other necessities that didn't belong in the living quarters. On this particular trip, there was a huge canvas tarpaulin up there that we used to cover our sixteen-foot skiff at night. Through some lapse in judgement, I had ordered it made up of heavy and expensive material.

I was plodding along a very narrow channel with oyster bars on each side when I met a squall. Even for the Everglades, this was a pretty fancy squall with an opaque downpour of rain and wind to very nearly stop me entirely. In the steering position, my head and shoulders were above the cabin, allowing my attention to be directed at the huge, irregular object coming at my head. It turned out to be the expensive and unused tarp from the foredeck. I thoughtfully grabbed for it as I ducked.

Afterwards I found myself clinging to the steering wheel spokes with one hand and a corner of the tarp with the other while the tarpaulin was standing straight out behind me in the wind and was pulling very hard indeed. Had I released it, I have no idea where it would have gone. Had I released the steering wheel, I knew I would have ended up on an oyster bar. Then the wind stopped, the tarp collapsed on the cockpit deck and *Bumboat* picked up her usual pedestrian speed. The sun came out brightly.

After a charter captain proved that for what it was costing to keep *Bumboat* afloat we could rent a cabin cruiser for weeks and live in luxury, we took a new look at the houseboat. I contemplated the fact that it had always leaked profusely, and that I had learned to pump a bilge while asleep. Finally, we decided to sell it. It was some time before we found a buyer, at a ruinous price.

As I recall, when the man wrote me the check for *Bumboat*, I drove off at high speed with the check in my teeth and never transferred it to my pocket until I was sure no one was following.

Chapter Twenty-Seven

MOTOR MADNESS

The big outboard sputtered and barely got us to the dock, and pushing on the steering wheel had little effect. Now and then the engine would quit entirely, and when I removed the cover I saw nothing recognizable except for the flywheel, several barely visible spark plugs, and a piece of starting rope for emergencies. In the past forty years motors have changed faster than I have.

I did not know a local outboard repairman, so I phoned a distant genius who recognizes all of those things under the hoods of engines and fixes a lot of the make that I was having trouble with.

"It's the fuel pump," he said. "Have somebody put on a new one made for last year's model."

"But how do you know it's the fuel pump?"

"Because," he answered calmly, "there is an 84 percent failure of the pump on that model and you have run it just the right length of time. Be sure you get the old model."

I have a policy about fishing in out-of-the-way places: use an engine that has relatives in the neighborhood. You'll be better off than I was the time I tried a brand-new make from Europe. As nearly as I can figure, mine was the only one ever built. All of the mechanics who looked at it thought it was wonderful workmanship and were sorry they had no parts for it. Unfortunately, an outboard motor is not properly shaped to be used as an anchor.

One thing I have noticed is that the farther you get from the big dealerships, the more resourceful the mechanics become. There have been several times when I have found myself at a pier a long way from home with a fishing day wearing on and a dead engine. I am impressed when someone is confident he can fix one.

Thirty years ago the man who owned the dock said he could, and settled down with a fistful of tools and an armful of colorful cardboard boxes. The boat was tied to the dock. I sat down in the bow, partly from an awe of outboard motor fixers and partly to keep from interrupting his train of thought. It was after I heard the fourth splash in the dockside water that I perked up. It seems the mechanic was taking off parts, throwing them away, and putting on new ones from the cardboard boxes. I asked him how he knew the parts were bad. He said he didn't but that he had no way to test them.

"I can put this stuff on pretty fast," he said. "You wanta' go fishing, don't you?"

There are little problems now and then, but things are better than they were before the days of gearshifts—especially in the case of larger motors, which had to be aimed before starting. I recall a resort owner who ran out on his pier, screaming at two startled fishermen, one of whom had his hand on the starting rope.

"Don't crank that damned thing in here!" yelled the proprietor. "Paddle it out fifty yards first." Later, he explained, "One of those things skinned up four boats and climbed the dock last week. "

Then there was the man standing waist deep in the water, waiting to catch a storage battery as his friend's boat passed him at high speed. "His battery's dead," he explained, "so he borrowed mine. His engine will run without a good battery but he can't crank it without one and he can't run slow because the engine won't idle."

Once our boat sank at a distant dock. We drained it and a local mechanic dismantled and dried out the engine, showing he had done such things before. Thinking of speed and oil mixtures, I asked how I should handle it now that it was purring.

"Handle it?" cried the mechanic. "Get rid of it! It won't last long!"

Chapter Twenty-Eight

THIN WATER

Although boats have been floating on shallow water for some time, the true "flats boat" has only recently come into its own. Just a few years ago a manufacturer told me there wasn't enough demand to make building them worthwhile; I suspect his staff is now working nights.

To really get into this we have to describe a flats boat's performance. We once thought a rig was running shallow if it went where things like a small heron or ibis were wading. Now it is necessary to describe a skiff that will run on a heavy dew or go where it looks like rain. The saltwater flats anglers got this started, and added the complication that whatever they used must be able to cross some choppy water—fast—to get to the barely wet places where things like bonefish or permit lived.

Those who choose to fish over the shallows must learn as much about bottoms as they know about water. And then some.

On sand bottom you usually grind to a stop pretty quickly, but it may not be a very long push back to water that floats you. Slick mud covered by grass is a completely different proposition—after you have slid fifty yards it suddenly occurs that you have a considerable wading push to get back to where you should not have left. Remember that a tide table is very important in such cases. It is always best to slide onto mud flats on an incoming tide—especially if you have no lunch aboard.

I was once caught on a falling tide—I won't go into detail but the wrinkled chart will show that we ran twenty-two miles in an area of Florida Bay where there wasn't supposed to be water. The boat was pretty heavy, the engine pretty potent, and as darkness fell we heard it take on a slightly different tune as it investigated soft bottom. If we'd let down, I doubt if we could have gotten up again that evening. I swore never again to travel over shallow water without a shovel to dig a trench with.

The true flats boat is a compromise and must take a little rough water. It is "quick out of the hole," which means it doesn't squat and dig when you gun it. A veteran shallow-water jockey learns to shove his throttle and swing his bow so that he levels off on his own wake. If it's a long way to deeper water he looks for the slightest bottom depressions up ahead and probably sweats a little.

Since a flats boat will make forays into the open sea, it needs a little bottom vee of one kind or another. I went with a guide who had no fear of the shallow places but had everyone on board sit on one gunwale so that we rode on the flat side of the vee. This is very tiresome after a few miles but is old hat to those who take boats where they aren't supposed to go. I do not find it in any Coast Guard safe-boating manuals.

Since tall fishermen had a decided advantage over short ones in seeing bonefish and the like at a distance, the kicker bridge—technically designated as the poling platform—

cropped up over the motor, and everyone had to get a longer pushpole. Note that it is farther to fall from the kicker bridge to the water and that what was once an embarrassing flub can now be a disaster. Before the kicker bridge, nearly everyone poled a boat backward, taking advantage of the streamlined bow and lifting the broad stern above the surface. Of course in recent years it is routine to install electric motors with foot controls on the platform (when pursuing skittish tarpon, the efficient guide looks like an amateur tap dancer) and use the pole simply to steer the rig.

I have been a student of falling polers. When we poled from the main boat deck, and the pole's "foot" stuck or slipped, it was common to do a rather sloppy fall over the side, hopeful that the water was deep enough to avoid contusions. Saltwater polers greatly admired canoe polers of the North who scooted around in a craft some anglers wouldn't even stand up in. With the advent of high kicker bridges, the poler has become an artist in the impromptu dive, and judges with numbered cards are all the scene lacks to make it a major athletic event. Over three feet of water can usually be handled headfirst and smoothly. Around eight inches of water and the poler must seek solid footing or carry a good insurance policy.

The purpose of the kicker bridge, however, was to enable the poler to see fish at a distance. Kicker bridges have added to the friction between polers and anglers, especially in the case of pushers who have been on the flats daily and anglers who haven't. It isn't a matter of eyesight, but a frustrated poler is likely to shriek a diagnosis of the angler's visual infirmities, forgetting he is perched several feet higher than the apparently blind caster.

In order to get the angler nearer to the poler's eye level, some casters began to pile things like coolers and tackle boxes on the boat's foredeck, occasionally falling off in the ensuing excitement. The evolution of the casting platform was the logical result.

Some of the more advanced flats boats present a rather strange silhouette, the casting platform—sometimes fenced in to keep the caster aboard approaching the height of the poler's perch. With the poler on his elevated deck and the caster on his, a fly line tangled in the tipped-up outboard motor becomes a major complication. To prevent that, various forms of barriers have been constructed, presenting a truly unusual look.

I've traveled carefully over shallow water most of the time, but there was once when grumpy fatigue caused me to show off. The end of an all-day saltwater Everglades fishing trip found us at low tide shortly before dusk. Before us, a soft and oozy mud flat was exposed for much of its breadth. Several outboards were waiting idly for the tide to rise—all seemingly drowsily resigned to a long wait.

With a bit of uncharacteristic showoff, I eyed the waterless space, recalled that the mud was very soft, and drew back some distance with a heavy-built, sixteen-footer that had plenty of outboard engine. I aimed at the nearest deep water on the other side, pushed the throttle all the way, prayed for the water pump, and clenched the steering wheel. With a geyser of muddy water falling behind us and on us, she switched a little but she went. Strangely, the abused water pump threw clean water as we reached the other side. I looked back at the waiting boats we had left and no one was napping. It was all stupid and wonderful.

Chapter Twenty-Nine

SMALLWOOD STORIES

I am going to get the Capone story out of the way first because I think I have it straight now. I had heard some other versions, and stories do change with the years. I never did hear Capone's side of it.

Since this will be Ted Smallwood's version, I have to explain a little about him. The fact is that Smallwood keeps getting into the picture because he is not exactly your run-of-the-mill legend, and I have known him for a long time.

Of course Smallwood is unusual because he lived in an unusual place at an unusual time. He was a fishing guide and boat captain down in the Ten Thousand Islands country of southwestern Florida, both before and after it became Everglades National Park.

People act a mite differently in wilderness country and near wilderness country—places where Al Capone didn't really belong, if he ever belonged anywhere except in prison, where he became a sick man and paid for income tax evasion.

Capone, I gather, wasn't too much of an angler, but you must remember that in his heyday Ten Thousand Island country was the most remote place that could be reached quickly from Miami.

Young Ted Smallwood was guiding (and in those days he wore white ducks on his spotless cruiser). He guided some very famous and very rich people, some of whom he didn't even know were rich or famous. Al Capone, who trolled from Smallwood's boat, used another name. On that trip he was accompanied by a pair of hard knockers that Smallwood noted immediately as not being ribbon salesmen. But Smallwood, wearing considerable bark himself, was not inclined to quiver uncontrollably at the sight of muscle.

It seems Capone was trolling while Ted swung his boat tight against the mangrove shoreline—an art less frequently practiced now but still seen occasionally. A big snook struck just as the lure swung near a downed tree. Ted saw that the snook would dive right into the tangle before the fisherman could crank it out so he gunned the engine (standard practice) and the fish broke off.

Capone, not particularly well versed in the aesthetics of angling, thought he had been jobbed and emitted some explicit language referring to Smallwood's antecedents, a reference Smallwood took immediate exception to. Smallwood neared Capone promptly but stopped his approach when confronted by the two anonymous companions of the fisherman who had not called himself Capone.

Each of the associates of the man who had not called himself Capone was pointing a large-caliber pistol with the attitude of one who could and would use it. Note that the fishing party was in the usual predicament of anglers who find themselves far from a dock in the Everglades with the sudden desire to terminate the employment of their guide. They had to get back and the boat was in the midst of a sort of jigsaw puzzle made of mangrove trees and brackish water.

The presence of the handguns encouraged a cessation of hostilities, and in the ensuing arbitration it was concluded that the man who had not up to that time called himself Mr.

Capone had been hasty in his criticism of his skipper. It was also decided that although Capt. Smallwood had been hasty in his response, he was still captain of the boat. After that, the well-known Chicago businessman gave Smallwood a bit of fatherly advice concerning tempers and corpses, and although he was later to be reticent before various courts of law, he described to Smallwood the details of the first murder he had committed and summarized a great many other demises in which he had been instrumental.

Now how much effect all of this had on the young Smallwood's temperament I do not know, but all of it is worth mentioning because very few shouldery young swamp rats with the nickname of Rooster have had paternal guidance from Al Capone. I guess this is about as straight as I can get the story.

Anyway Smallwood, who was sometimes called Biff as well as Rooster, was long noted for settling disagreements directly, one of the more recent occasions involving several employees of an automobile agency where his car was smashed while being taken to the service department after Smallwood had requested that he be allowed to drive it there himself. I think the pertinent part of that episode is the salutation by one of the Miami policemen who soon arrived at the red-spattered scene of discord. He asked, "What on earth is going on here, Captain Ted?"

Ted was pretty well known then, but has been gone for several years and there's no reason for being secretive about his antics now. There is no Rooster to start discussions with his big paw twisted in somebody's shirt front. And I am inclined to feel that although he may have responded a bit hastily, I can't say he was often in the wrong. Of course, some of it was for fun.

Automobiles have figured in several Smallwood stories, and if you had seen him slide up in the tasteful sedans of his later days you would never suspect him of building a thinly disguised tank for driver education purposes.

Ted wanted to visit Alaska with his family, and since I had done some hunting and fishing up there he discussed the trip with me. I don't think he listened too well when I told him that the long road was filled with gravel and stones, which were inclined to break headlights and windshields when thrown by hurrying trucks.

Ted went up the long road with a neat pickup camper. The truckers not only cracked considerable glass and dented a lot of sheet metal for him, but they also caused a leak that let the highway dirt in where Ted's new shotgun was riding and disrupted the Smallwood housekeeping in general. When he reached Alaska, Ted simply turned around and headed back. Sightseeing and fishing could wait, for he had more important things to do.

The fact is he assembled a very expensive and practical Alaska Highway vehicle. It took the better part of a year and involved a specially equipped truck with a heavy-duty camper body, and I watched stages of the construction with wide-eyed apprehension. No expense was spared and I kept thinking back to the mechanized cavalry of World War II. Some of the parts were imported from other states and I think the engine was modified in Texas.

Ted invited me to take a ride in his rig when he was finishing it and I got aboard late one evening when there was no traffic. We turned smoothly into a stretch of vacant highway and the gears changed softly, accompanied by a guttural rumble somewhere in the depths. Within a mile the guttural rumble had become somewhat louder, and the speedometer showed ninety-five miles an hour. Nothing rattled or vibrated, and Ted said he thought things were pretty well adjusted.

The drill that summer on the way to Alaska was to travel like any other family of tourists until one of those highballing truckers headed for Anchorage or Fairbanks would come by too fast and throw too many rocks. Then there was a standard procedure. Ted used it when a big Peterbilt diesel with all those wheels rattled rocks on an ideally hilly section of the road, bouncing some of them off Ted's RV hood.

"I waited until he was headed uphill so my tires would dig," Ted explained. "Then I passed him, downshifted, and dropped her in the nine-hole. In the mirror I could see big white spots showing where the rocks busted his windshield, and when he threw his arms up over his face I knew I had him."

It was a wonderful summer. The "nine-hole," incidentally, is the last notch on the throttle of an old-time shrimp boat.

Ted is not always the hero of his own stories. I like the Broad River swimming bit about as well as any. Broad River is

one of the prettiest of the tidal streams on the lower Florida west coast between Lostman's and Shark rivers. With normal water runoff its upper stretches are completely fresh instead of brackish.

Years ago, when Smallwood was using a live-aboard cruiser for his fishing parties down there, he'd tow a couple of skiffs for fishing. After the day's operation he'd often run up toward the head of Broad, and the whole party would go swimming.

Now I've changed the names and addresses to protect the guilty but the facts are right, Ted says.

It seems that Ted was not ashamed of his physique in those days, and he was not above playing a little rough with some of his regular clients. Like Mr. Perkins of Chicago. When

Perkins would come down with his guests and they'd anchor at the head of Broad for the evening swimming party, Perkins had a habit of offering a hundred dollars to the last man left on the cruiser. Ted found this a source of considerable spending money and especially enjoyed chucking Perkins over. Evidently Perkins became a little tired of finding himself and his guests in Broad River with Ted still on deck.

There was the time when Perkins brought his daughter and her girlfriend on a fishing trip and when they anchored at the head of Broad, Ted said, "I picked up old Perkins and chucked him into the river. Then I looked around and picked up his daughter, who was kind of pretty, and I threw her into the river kind of slow. Then I looked around and there was her pretty girlfriend lying on deck and saying she didn't want to go into the water.

" 'It's your turn though, honey,' I said, and I reached for her. Next thing I knew I was standing on my head on the bottom of Broad River. That old skunk had brought a female judo expert all the way from Chicago!"

Few of the disagreements deep in the backcountry are as serious as the one with the Capone party, but one of them involved a nationally famous football coach who was there as a guest of one of Ted's regular clients. The coach wasn't doing too well fishing, and when the host would hook a tarpon, the coach would toss a lure across his line and break it. Big joke. Ted announced he'd put Coach overboard if it happened again. It did and he did.

The coach swam to a small island so far away from a dock that civilization was just a memory and refused to apologize. He didn't have many clothes and the mosquitoes were bad. Ted and the other man settled down on the cruiser for the night not far from the island, and the host pleaded with Ted to go back for Coach. Ted went back in the skiff but couldn't get a suitable apology at first. Finally, the Everglades mosquitoes settled the issue and a grunting apology came out, but it was a slit-eyed and guarded trip from then on.

The swamps down there have become considerably modernized in recent years but shreds of direct-action attitudes remained for a long time.

Take Chop-In Creek. Wimpy Steerman and I were poking through a canopied mangrove tidal stream, making short underhand casts with plugs beneath the mangrove branches. A snook came and got my darter and dived down into what at first appeared to be a disorganized pattern of sunken logs. But it wasn't.

I looked down through the dark but clear water where my darter had gone and blinked when I saw that the tree trunks were lying in orderly parallels, crosswise of the creek. They'd been cut in some bygone year and had gradually rotted and sunk until they resembled a submerged corduroy road. What for?

"Aw, that's Chop-In Creek," the man said back at Chokoloskee. "Nobody liked so-and-so much, so one day when he ran his boat up that creek to some little bays, some of the boys chopped him in so he couldn't run back out. That's been done now and then in this country."

Maybe he chopped out as he had been chopped in. The snook never did give back my plug.

It was a different law back in the swamp. The white ibis have come back greatly in recent years and flocks of them flare upward when they find you fishing a narrow creek as they fly low to beat the wind on their way to roost. They were getting pretty scarce for a while.

But you can still hear them "shooting a roost" back in the swamp on some quiet evenings. I guess "Everglades chicken" remains a tradition in some families. If you keep a little of the good old days, you get a little of the bad old days with it.

Maybe I should mention that Ted Smallwood helped put some other folks' kids through college. Probably wouldn't have admitted it. A man has an image to maintain.

Chapter Thirty

A MATTER
OF MANNERS

Since neither Emily Post nor Miss Manners has given much attention to the matter of fishing and hunting etiquette, I feel it is essential that I attempt to forestall the occasional crudities cropping up in the boondocks and on the high seas.

For example, when operating a high-speed bass boat in shallow water, it is bad form to run over wading fishermen, even though they sometimes use cheap tackle and seek panfish.

When piloting a good-sized cruiser that pulls a tall wake, your thoughtful skipper always keeps several extra boat cushions or life jackets on hand to throw to capsized canoeists or users of inflated float tubes. If in a hurry he can always recover them later at the morgue or Coast Guard station.

Ever since steel shot has been made mandatory in waterfowl areas, there have been questions about its use, and some anglers have inquired as to whether it is mandatory with regard to jet skiers. I do not consider this a serious question for, after all, jet skiers seem to be fellow human beings despite numerous arguments to the contrary.

The subject of flats fishing by fly rodders in salt water invariably brings up protocol involving bonefish skiffs that have guides on their poling platforms. At this point it must be understood that there is a class of immortal Florida Keys guides who must not be judged by the same standards used for people. To a lesser degree, this also applies to guides on various tropical islands and coasts far south of Florida.

These beings must be handled with due humility since anyone who argues with one of them might be beaten with a pushpole in an afterlife. Although I have an acquaintance who has developed a method of removing a poler from a platform through a deft backcast with a twelve-weight fly line and a 4/0 streamer, I have never encountered anyone with the courage to reduce the exorbitant tip expected by flats guides. That would be unheard-of bad form.

In submitting to criticism from flats guides, it must be remembered the phrases used by them toward clients have been polished through long study of the language used by boatswain's mates and camel drivers. It is bad form to mention that a tall man on a high platform should be able to see a bonefish from farther away than a short woman standing at water level in the bow.

Tact is really another term for good manners. In the embarrassing situation of having seen an approaching fish before one's guide sights it, there are several approaches, but probably the best is to say:

"Captain, do I see a little nervous water out there at eleven o'clock? (You say this even though you can plainly see a nine-pound bonefish out there and could count his scales if there were any need for it.)

The guide's response is probably, "Yeah, I've been watching that and make it a bonefish plain as day. Start casting."

Of course if a fish flushes before he sees it, the guide can explain it was only a small ray and that he has been watching it for some time. Then the client says he can't understand how the guide can read the water so well and the guide admits that it is a matter of practice, superhuman eyesight, and superior intellect.

There are special etiquette standards for guides. If you don't see a tarpon at two o'clock (by the routine method of "clock location,") the truly proper guide will ask you courteously if you ever learned to tell time rather than calling you names generally heard only in prison exercise yards and on cable TV. Never lose your head as a friend of mine did and call him the seventh son of a noseless goat herder. He will expect a bigger tip.

A true sportsman never trolls between a caster and the shoreline—if the caster is closer than forty feet from the edge. This is difficult for many fishermen to understand, especially those who love their fellow man and feel all recreation is a social matter. An example of this little *faux pas* was put before me recently when an electric motor jockey moved between us and a shoreline. He was only thirty feet away when he cut us off, and in the interests of science I cast a popping bug across his bow, retrieving about four feet ahead of it. He stared down at the bug with clinical interest and studied its progress as I twitched it in. I asked him if we were getting in his way (after all, the lake is only nine miles long) and he displayed true sportsmanship.

"Why, of course not!" he said graciously. "You fish around here all you want to!"

Basically, your true sportsman is deeply chivalrous toward the opposite sex and I think of the couple fishing from a skiff along a shoreline using live bait. Things were quiet for a while and then the lady had a hard strike, causing her to gasp, lean on the rod, and say, "Lookit 'im go!"

Her husband, obviously fearing she might strain her wrists, grabbed the rod, said "Gimme that! That's a big red!" and shoved her over backward on the seat of her pants. Not understanding she had been saved from possible injury, the lady complained that her fish had been taken away from her.

Real men know a woman's place and understand when to step in for their protection. I learned this long ago, since my wife fishes a great deal and there have been many instances when total strangers have rushed to her aid. There was the time when she was wading deep into a Yellowstone Park trout stream and was catching quite a few trout when two sportsmen saw she was standing in a dangerous depth. They rushed over and cast across her line from both sides, causing her to seek safety on the bank, saving her from possible drowning in case the river rose suddenly.

Some of the least-mentioned points of etiquette are practiced during hunting, and these are especially important when hunting dogs are involved. Good friends frequently seek upland birds while working their dogs together, and all hunters should be aware of the traditional bond between a hunter and his dog. It has been said that a man who is moderate in his views on flag burning and is willing to accept slighting remarks about his wife is likely to fly into a towering rage upon hearing derogatory remarks about Old Spot.

This requires some explanation since he is, himself, likely to call Old Spot x-rated names and may state regularly that Spot is an accident of misguided ancestry. He may insist that in a long career of bird dog ownership he has never encountered an example of such canine imbecility. However, even though Old Spot may chase deer, roll in deceased skunks, eat birds instead of retrieving them, and raid barnyard chicken coops, his owner will take umbrage instantly at the first slighting remark by a hunting companion.

Although I am aware of this, there are some occasions upon which I may forget my manners and say something mildly critical when my associate's dog performs some particularly heinous crime. In this case, I find the most conciliatory move is to immediately pick up something and hit my own dog, whether he has done anything wrong or not. This tends to cloud the issue so much that even a senior Congressman would forget the original attack upon Old Spot's character.

There is a special bit of etiquette involving dove shooters who have retrievers that bring all of the birds killed within sight of their owner's stand, regardless of who shoots them. When the shoot is over, the true gentleman sportsman will cull over the retrieved doves and, after picking the plumpest and least damaged limit for himself, will offer the remaining birds to other shooters on a first-come, first-served basis.

Safety is, of course, the number one consideration in all kinds of firearms sport, and when you are continually looking down the muzzle of your associate's gun it is wise to either mention the hazard or seek a new friend. I hunted with a fine shot who habitually carried his autoloading shotgun over his shoulder in such a way that when he was ahead of me the muzzle unerringly pointed between my eyes.

Chapter Thirty-One

WOMEN OF THE WILDS

In this definitive study of the female fisher and/or hunter it is essential to point out certain attitudes of the male hunter and/or fisher with regard to the female. After more than forty years of direct contact with lady casters and shooters, I feel these attitudes are best shown through specific examples:

A deep slough lies just off a famous spring creek in the West and it has contained some big trout who seem to have retired there to avoid the hustle and bustle of current and splashy little fish. For some years my wife Debie had maintained a rapport with those recluses, having released a number of them after rather exciting scuffles. The slough is quite deep and full of vegetation and Debie generally used a float tube to keep her chin above water.

Now the slough water was very clear and cold. Debie would sight a corpulent citizen nosing slowly among the underwater towers of algae, would figure his route, and would carefully cast a very small surface terrestrial where she guessed the trout was going. In a surprising number of cases the trout would accept with a dimple what Debie had tied up and the ensuing battle would often cause mallards to squawk and leave from around a bend. Debie broke off most of them but she caught and released her share. She tried to teach me to do it but I was a little short on patience and I was inclined to watch her from a little bluff, which I was doing when the nice man came along.

The Nice Man was wearing a felt hat with some of those little medallions telling where he had fished and hunted and his vest had some club patches. His cane rod had been made on purpose and his wading shoes were good leather. He stopped on the bank just a little above Debie's position.

Debie had been having a pretty busy morning. It was well into fall and she was getting chilly. Her stocking cap was yanked well below her ears and her nose was red. So were her fingers where they stuck out of her fishing gloves. She had taken a little water when she'd landed her last trout. I guess she didn't look too sharp as she tried to clean her fly and put a little dope on her line.

"Lady," said the Nice Man in the pleasant voice I'll bet he used when he lectured on fly tying at the university, "you can't catch these fish in here. You have to go over there to the creek proper where the water is fast."

"Oh," said Debie. "Gee, these looked so big and slow I fig-ured they'd be easier. Thanks for the tip."

"You're welcome," said the Nice Man with a tolerant chuckle. "Glad to help."

The Nice Man walked on toward the creek and Debie blew on her fingers and then on her fly. She sniffed his pipe smoke, and asked if he had gone. He had, I said from the little bluff.

Debie made a cautious false cast and craned her neck.

"See that big clown over there by the cattails? I think I caught him last week. Watch this!"

My wife Debie gets into my rantings a lot because I have watched her fish and shoot for a long time. She casts pretty well and ties sloppy and nameless but productive flies. She can't shoot a shotgun but gets rather poisonous when hunkered down with a .280 rifle. She fired in a lot of pistol matches and was beaten by a number of women shooters. She camps happily where I would die of exposure and starvation. If she were a man she would be neither scorned nor heralded as an outdoorsman. As it is, she bears the lady sport's cross.

Outdoor persons should be judged individually, regardless of sex. At a long-ago big skeet shoot, which I attended as a reporter, I was a trifle miffed when those in charge turned me over to a ravishing beauty who would handle the public relations. She would help me follow the scene. I was dazzled but I had hoped for the aid of a shooter who would discuss guns and scores. Still, it was not the lady's fault and I made conversation, finally getting a little expansive while she listened big-eyed.

"Of course," I said, "the real small bores cannot compete with the 20s and 12s."

"Well, gee, I don't know," said Miss America. "I won the 28 with a hundred straight at Phoenix last week."

I saw a youthful Debie at a loss for words when she appeared in a photograph with a large snook which she caught in Everglades country. The enlarged photo was displayed in a tackle shop and once when Debie was present, the proprietor pointed out to customers that she was the one holding the fish. One asked her if she had caught it, whereupon there were gales of laughter. It had never occurred to Debie that there was doubt of that. She favored the group with a poisonous glare and walked out.

A lady shopper for hard sporting goods has communication problems. A long time ago, at a time when five feet was the fairly standard length for baitcasting rods, Debie entered a San Francisco sporting goods store to buy a six-footer. Now she had chosen the six-foot length after careful consideration and testing. Debie doesn't skimp on rods and she figured a really light six-footer for half-ounce baits would be just the thing for some black bass plotting she had been doing. Okay, my wife is a little kinky for rods.

The clerk told her she did not need or want a six-foot rod.

"You don't understand, lady," he said. "This is a rod and not a pole. Having it real long does not make the bait go out that much farther. You see, the line rolls off the reel."

He was getting exasperated. *HE* was getting exasperated!

Debie has listened to a great deal of advanced stuff around salty fishing docks. While making adjustments on some saltwater fly tackle, including some tall rods with a lot of line on them, she was approached by a kindly do-gooder who told here that she should have her husband get her a push-button spinning outfit. Those long poles, he explained, were for perch and bluegills. But then, she'd been told on another occasion that the nine-weight fly line (fifteen-pound leader) "looked like a hundred pounds" and that the real fishermen were using nothing heavier than thirty-five or forty.

When she was shooting regularly in NRA handgun matches she had a little problem with gun shops if she entered alone. At one time she concluded that in the .22 matches she could do better with a customized old-style Colt Woodsman, and since the older models had pretty well disappeared from the shelves at that time, she took a picture of one with her and went into various shops in hope of finding one in mint condition.

The clerks, a little confused by a lady handgun shopper, would glance at the picture, note that it was an autoloading pistol, and try to sell Debie one of those little pearl-handled .25-caliber jobs, which they assured her would fit much better in her purse. If anybody cares, Debie did finally get just what she wanted, spent more than she could afford on customization, and used it in pistol matches for several years.

Before women's hunting and fishing clothing spruced up recently, Debie was fairly successful in the boys' department but didn't do too well with some items. Even in this day of chic outdoor clothing there is an occasional surprise. Debie's hunting boots were coming apart and last summer she went to a sharp-looking shoe store in a South Dakota mall. It bore the name of a famous line of boots that have stomped half a century of mountains. She asked for hunting boots and the sales lady came up with some pretty sharp ones. They were quite high, fur-lined, and zipper closed—fur around the tops and with spike heels. Debie said they weren't quite what she had in mind and the lady said the fall styles might be different.

The wader business has changed very rapidly and there are advertising photos of athletic young ladies doing aerial splits in the latest models. There was a time when Debie had trouble getting waders she could see out of. Then she painstakingly ordered a custom-built pair. After all, we could miss a few meals for something really important. They fit pretty well. They leaked very badly. But since the boondocks became stylish, women's hunting and fishing clothing is becoming expensively attractive. I can recall when it was hard to pry a woman hunter away from sneakers because she would announce in awed tones that for the price of a pair of Russell Birdshooters she could get a really nice pair of spectator pumps.

For one thing, women seldom seem to dote on valued sporting gear. Some of the finest lady marksmen can be extremely vague about their guns—enough to make some questioners wonder if they are just a little phony. I have seen marvelous lady trout anglers who hadn't the slightest idea of their rod and line specifications, and although some of the finest fly tyers are women, the ladies who use the flies are inclined to forget their names. My wife carries hundreds of tiny trout flies in aluminum boxes, many of them tied by herself, but she knows the names of only a few.

She used to be a pretty good deer hunter and used two bolt-action rifles—a .280 and a .243. She had killed at least three muleys with heads bigger than any I ever shot, but she quit hunting a few years back and her knowledge of rifles evaporated. She now holds one like a vacuum sweeper and has to check the marking on the barrel to tell which is the .280, although at one time she insisted that the stock be exactly the right length. Ladies, most of you don't talk a very good game.

Women sports have been treated unkindly by the media. Admittedly, there are more hotshot men fishers and hunters than there are women topnotchers. More men hunt and fish.

Women anglers are likely to be the subjects of all sorts of cutesy compliments. I recall an outdoor writer who rhapsodized over the deep-wading steelhead caster who attached her own flies and strung up her own rod. This did not flatter the lady, who managed to tie on the flies herself but also constructed them from scratch for both herself and her husband.

Lady fishing experts who feel slighted can have the attitude of a sack of cobras. I once wrote something about women anglers in which I complained that a few famous ones had gotten that way by sitting in offshore fighting chairs while the real fish-finding and other details were handled by captains and mates. The result was a deluge of acid letters from women anglers who did everything themselves, and the magazine editor hinted broadly that I might be in the wrong line of work. He was especially impressed by telephone calls from overseas. For a while I kept and answered the letters forwarded to me. I believe the longest critique was from the lady skipper of an offshore cruiser who used up seven pages, single spaced, without repeating herself. For a while I considered changing my name, but it was too late to change hobbies to rugby or surfing. If I had needed a new name, the women had submitted a considerable variety for selection.

Ladies operate under a male-imposed handicap. For example, if a woman catches a larger fish than her husband does, it is a real leg-slapper in many quarters. Except where physical strength is important, as with big tuna or billfish, I have always wondered why a woman shouldn't catch as big a fish as a man does. My wife has caught several black bass bigger than any I've landed and several snook bigger than mine. I have caught bigger trout, tarpon, and steelhead, but we sure never made any announcements on the subject.

I was watching a superb fly fisherman the other day and was standing by his wife, who is also very, very good at it. I remarked at how pretty the caster's line looked and how delicately the fly alighted. She was equally admiring of it, and I mentioned that she had similar technique to her husband's. Maybe, I said, she was better at the delicacy part. She flustered a little.

"I don't want to fish as well as he does," she said, "and I sure don't want to fish *better* than he does.

Why not? See, you women have a problem.

Chapter Thirty-Two

SNAKE PHILOSOPHY

"Snakes," my old hunting buddy said, "are part of nature's balance. I would never harm any kind of snake."

At the moment, we were being interviewed by a large eastern diamondback rattler and it seemed that his eyes were almost on a level with mine. Since twelve-foot rattlesnakes are very scarce, even in Florida, it is possible he wasn't coiled quite that high. I fingered my safety and contemplated what would have been my course of action if we'd been hunting somewhere else, but I was a guest and the other guy managed the property.

The bird dogs stood well back. The rattler sounded like a stage-full of Spanish dancers with castanets. I suggested that snakes eat a lot of bird eggs. My friend said that they also eat a lot of rodents and things balance out. I suggested that he shoots a lot of quail every year, and in cooperation with the snake he was putting a kink in Mother Nature's balance.

My friend said that he was very considerate in his friendship for snakes. Why, he said, five of his dogs had been nailed by various unappreciative rattlesnakes, but that was only the balance of nature at work and the dogs generally got well anyway. Not wishing to meddle too much in Mother Nature's business myself, I checked my snake boots and walked away backwards.

"Snakes hardly ever bite you," my friend explained and I explained to him that I did not want snakes to bite me *at all*. At the time, I had just finished what I had hoped would be a definitive article for hunters and fishermen regarding poisonous snakes. In doing that I had done considerable study and had come up with a few hard facts, some of which were disturbing. For example, there was the mathematics regarding a snake's striking range. The experts disagreed on almost everything, but all of them concluded that a snake could strike for at least two-thirds of its length.

I then licked a pencil and figured carefully that a six-foot rattler sunning himself beside a country road would be quite capable of hitting you as you drove past in your sports car with the top down. The figure works equally well for either German or Japanese cars. This has never been done, possibly because no snake has ever thought of it.

But snakes are not necessarily cowed by motorized transportation. A friend of mine was tooling his jeep along a back road two-track when he felt a jar as if someone had whacked the rig with a club. He backed up, got out to look, and found a big rattler glaring at one of his rear tires. I am tempted to say that the tire went flat but it didn't. See, I'm sticking to the truth.

Like most ancients, I was reared where all snakes were considered enemies of mankind and even a little green garden snake was likely to get belted with a hoe. A great many fishermen used to carry handguns in their tackle boxes "for snakes." Actually, the firepower was employed in a variety of plinking, which prevented crowding by other anglers.

I do not favor the practice, for a friend of mine had a snake complex, and when a surprised water moccasin lost its grip and fell into my friend's boat from an overhanging branch, he became disturbed, yanked open his tackle box, and opened fire with his .45-caliber automatic—Model 1911—while a companion at the other end of the boat yelled warnings. My friend with the heater could shoot fast, but Wild Bill Hickok he was not. He did not damage the snake, but he made the bottom of the boat look like the ventilated end of a bird dog shipping crate. Only shortly afterward it was decided to abandon ship, leaving the skiff to the water moccasin. It was full of water anyway.

Nothing brings forth snake experts as quickly as a crowd of onlookers. Long ago, when traffic was very light in Florida, my wife and I came upon a small traffic jam caused by a really big rattlesnake on the highway. All present thought the snake should be killed, and one fellow tried to do so by running over it with his 1951 Chevrolet. Although this didn't seem to injure the snake seriously, it did cause the snake to take umbrage, and his rattle sounded like a war dance on a tin roof. To use a term currently popular, this was one big sucker.

A man got out of a car and asked if anyone present had anything to hit the snake with. I could tell instantly that he knew a lot about a lot of things. I had a bumper jack and he said any little heavy thing would do to swat the rattler into rattler heaven. I handed him the jack and he walked over, wound up, and tried to bring the jack down on the snake's head. As he teed off, the reptile decided the hazard was not really the jack but the guy swinging it (they say a snake senses heat, and the jack was cold). The snake did at least the standard two-thirds of his length in the strike, and he was a very long snake. He missed the snake expert but the expert left him with my bumper jack and I had to wait until the snake left to get it. After the rattler went into the roadside weeds, the traffic began to move again.

Snake stories grow faster than snakes and there has been a rumor of some tropical snakes with heads three feet wide. I hope there aren't very many of them, as that would make Crocodile Dundee look like a hamster hunter. But after sifting through the rumors in primitive countries, Roger Caras stated in a book on dangerous creatures that there are between 30,000 and 40,000 people killed annually by snakes. Caras said some of the constrictors get thirty feet long, but that they aren't as dangerous as poisonous snakes that specialize in biting.

In the United States, less than 2 percent of the people struck by poisonous snakes are likely to die, but even those odds are not satisfactory for real snake respecters. The late Ross Allen, demonstrative herpetologist, used to have little scars all over his arms where he had "made mistakes," as he said.

When I researched my snake piece I was pretty receptive to snake information and found that the snake-bite experts were divided into warring factions. They recommended completely different forms of snake bite treatment. I was really sold on one of those experts until he explained carefully that there are no sea snakes that will harm anybody, but I've heard from serious students that the most deadly snakes in the world live in salt and brackish water.

Hunting dogs are regular targets of both rattlers and water moccasins, and all sorts of sneaky devices have been figured out for snakeproofing dogs. The first I ever saw was made up of a box containing a rattlesnake skin and a dry-cell battery. Its inventor ran deer dogs and his treatment was to get the snake skin moving. When Rover grabbed it, my friend would give the dog enough electricity to light up St. Louis. After he came around, old Rover would have an abiding distaste for all snakes, regardless of species. However, the original rig was not fully developed and the operator frequently got enough jolt to cross his eyes.

When the electric collar was developed we had a beautiful snakeproofing unit as well as a form of instant punishment when a dog did something really bad, such as chasing a rancher's cattle into the Columbia River or attacking a mailman bearing Social Security checks. When Jack and I got our first electric collar, Jack said it should be tested as he didn't want to use anything that was really harmful to his pointer.

"I shall get George to help me test it tonight," Jack said.

I did not know why Jack needed help to test the collar, but it developed that the test was a surprise to George, who was holding and admiring it when Jack pushed the button. Jack said it worked fine but that maybe we shouldn't mention the test to George as Jack had told George it was an accident.

Jack said he had paid special attention to George, whose hair appeared to stand on end during the test. One thing worried Jack, though. He mentioned that George weighed 250 pounds and maybe the same shock would be pretty hard on a dog. But the collar did work great. We would show the dog a snake in a pen, and when Old Spot got really curious we'd light him up with the electric collar. A more refined system was used by people who would let a dog get really familiar with a defanged snake and then push the button. The result was that any time you met a bird dog running fast in the wrong direction, it was likely he had heard rumors of a snake up ahead.

They tell me that no natural dislike of snakes is built into humans and that snake fear is a learned reaction. Most of us don't get the horrors at first view. There are, of course, some folks who can walk on water, fly from ridges, and climb sheer walls at the sight of a lowly corn snake. Snakes, I understand, have had a favorable effect on alcoholism.

Charles Askins, a noted hunter and gun authority, has a reputation for enjoying danger and liked to hunt in Asia where there were king cobras. He said that when a king cobra reared his head up above a stand of brush and you couldn't tell which way he intended to go, it was quite a thrill that added all sorts of spice to a big-game hunt. Since one irritable king cobra could wipe out the Dallas Cowboy offensive line, this is pretty heady nature study.

I once went quail hunting somewhere in Mexico and the birds were there by the thousands, but the country was nothing but thornbushes and it was almost impossible to make the birds fly. The dusty ground had millions of quail tracks and it looked as if someone had been rolling a truck tire around the place. I finally asked what made that mark and learned there were quite a few constrictors in the neighborhood. Sure spiced up the hunt.

For years, a bunch of us pistol nuts used to shoot rats at night at the South San Francisco city dump, and hotshot pistoleros came from miles around to blast away at rats hurrying over the tin cans, illuminated by big flashlights. Then there was a big grass fire in the neighborhood and they found the burned-out skeleton of a huge snake. We never knew if it had escaped from an animal show or if it had arrived as a youth on one of the banana boats that docked nearby. It did, however, spice up the rat shooting. In fact, it was so spicy that most of us lost interest in walking around there in the dark.

The Guinness Book of World Records needed a piece on the time I accidentally met the residents of one of those big rattlesnake dens I'd always thought were folk tales. They were sunning themselves after a chilly night and I found there were six of them within five feet of my boots. The record part was the fifty feet I moved without touching the ground, carrying a medium-weight shotgun.

I have never liked to sleep in those Everglades shacks where they keep maintenance serpents on the loose to control rats and mice, especially on cool nights when a four-foot rat snake is looking for a warm spot.

Chapter Thirty-Three

TENT
TRAUMAS

Those who spend considerable time camping in the boondocks learn to accept unusual sights. They never confess to insomnia, which is a malady of the tenderfoot.

As an example, I cite the ancient who had actually hunted buffalo and lived in what was simply known as "Indian Country," where numerous large beasties were known to hold forth. I confess to being old enough to have been around during the last of his hundred or so years, during which time he lived in houses with various descendants. Some of them were not above playing an occasional joke on the old codger. One such incident occurred when he fell asleep on a divan shortly after some sort of family dinner. There was one youthful wiseguy who had learned to emit a blood-curdling scream, remindful of African carnivores and football fans.

With a lot of tip-toeing and hushing, the whole crowd sneaked in to where they could watch old John's response when the family smart-aleck delivered his scream a foot from the old man's ear. The scream was a real hair-lifter, sounding like a tomcat's squall delivered from a boombox.

Old John didn't fully wake up. He just shifted his position slightly on the divan and said: "Bert! Git up! They's a panther in the tent!"

That was spoken like a true camper who considers catastrophe routine. His type doesn't lose sleep until something really important happens.

In telling the privations of hunting and fishing camping, it is a temptation to branch into the experiences of service personnel in wartime. However, since these tend to overshadow sporting experiences, I do not include them. I was impressed by an old fishing friend of mine who doesn't want to camp at all.

"I am not seeking a new camping experience," he said. "I once camped over much of Europe and the weather was not very good. My scoutmaster was named Georgie Patton."

Anyway, I restrict my account to those trips made for pleasure, some of which employ techniques similar to those of the military. When engaged in pleasure, it is poor form to complain about anything. In the service, it's poor form not to complain about everything.

There is a great deal of drama in tents. As youths seeking adventure during the Great Depression, several of us found ourselves without funds or freight trains in a small Colorado town. I think it was Alamosa, but a more recent check does not reveal the exact locale of my narrative. There was a little lake with a small pier and a public campground next to it. The lake contained numerous carp weighing around six or eight pounds and while fishing for them was prohibited, we were quite hungry and felt a nocturnal urge for food.

So we rigged a husky fishing outfit, chummed up the carp under the single pier light-bulb, and one of us managed to lasso one of the fish, giving it a great heave. The fish landed atop a big wall tent that had been pitched at the land end of the little pier and flopped wildly. There were several tent occupants and they began to escape without seeking the door.

As I ran with the fish in my arms (getting scratched up in a barbed wire fence without letting it go) I had to look back at the tent, which gave forth strange sounds, bulging wildly and finally collapsing in a great convulsively twitching heap of canvas. Ever since then I have checked for the nearest exit when I have slept in a big tent.

Tent construction can be complex, and faulty materials can cause unique results. I once strayed into British Columbia to hunt with a large party of Stone-sheep seekers and the sports all slept in what was respectfully called the "dude tent," a huge pyramid-shaped nylon affair with plenty of room for more than our half-dozen sleeping bags and other personal gear.

There were rutting bull moose all over the place and a lovesick bull moose will approach almost anything he thinks is alive, seeking either romance or war. Doesn't seem to care which.

One night at a new campsite I heard some stamping and blowing outside the tent. Everyone else was asleep and I had no doubt what was going on. A bull moose had taken an interest in the big tent. He snorted and blew on one side and then on another and I kept wondering if he would come inside, but he didn't. Finally, he quieted down a little and I had dozed off when suddenly the tent fell down on top of us. It was only a broken rope, but in my stupor I assumed it was a moose and a bright orange map of warm, safe, civilized country flashed before me. But then, I suppose drunken drivers and muggers are as bad as moose.

It is common for campers to fear attacks by wild animals, but I am much more afraid of campers who are afraid of wild animals than I am of wild animals. Take the time we saw a black bear checking out our campground. Now black bears and grizzlies are very different, but a half-tame black bear is not to be fooled with, and the one in question was obviously a regular at looking for garbage or handouts in the public campground.

The bear was a little too bold to suit me and I mentioned him to some late arrivals who weren't using a tent, just putting down their sleeping bags. One of them said he wasn't worried and hauled out a Mannlicher, which he put down beside his bag. You see, I even noted the exact model of the rifle. There is something about a mixture of nightfall and bears that causes me to be attentive to detail.

The bear did not enter camp until after midnight. Displaying a healthy curiosity, he peered into the rifle owner's sleeping bag and woofed in surprise to find a man in there. It is difficult to get out of a fully-closed sleeping bag fast but the guy with the rifle did it pretty well. As it turned out, there were no bullet holes in anything, including the bear, but we didn't sleep much more that night. A large-caliber rifle is surprisingly loud in the darkness. The next morning, the bear's deeply dug high-speed tracks appeared two feet from where my head had been inside our tent.

I have not seen many grizzly bears, but the first fresh grizzly track I saw made an impression on me. I was alone somewhere in British Columbia and had been fishing for grayling in a chilly little creek. It was not an auspicious evening because I went over my hip boots and then burned holes in them while trying to dry them with hot rocks. I stuck some grayling on dingle sticks over a small fire, ate them and crawled into a sleeping bag and a little mountain tent. When I awoke the next morning I found a grizzly track near where my head had been all night. When I put my foot into the track, the full length of the claws extended past my toes. Ever since then I have been careful to distinguish between black bear stories and grizzly bear stories.

I learned sleeping bag travel in very cold weather while living in an old wall tent with a sheet-iron stove for heat. In those days all of the best sleeping bags were made with down and that was one place I didn't worry about economy. It has been said that some of the duck and goose shortages of those days were caused by the construction of my sleeping bags. The seat and knees of my hunting pants might be a little thin but there was plenty of down in my three sleeping bags.

When living in our old wall tent it was quite possible that interior temperatures would get somewhere between zero and ten above. When the alarm went off at 5:00 A.M., it was necessary for someone to stir up the coals and put some new wood on the fire. I learned to do this by humping along on the ground in my sleeping bag and getting the fire started with one arm at a time when I reached the stove. Then I'd crawl back a little and wait for the stove to turn red.

Show me a man who can't crawl in a sleeping bag and I'll show you a tenderfoot unworthy of association with outdoorsmen like me. Show me a man who just jumps out in his underwear and starts a fire that way and I'll show you another guy I don't want to associate with. He's a showoff who will probably get hypothermia.

While sleeping in a tent may have minor disadvantages, sleeping in a country barn can be a little spooky. Late on a stormy night I slipped off a country road in a driving rainstorm. I walked to a farmhouse and the nightshirted owner told me he'd help me get out the next morning. In the meantime, he said, I could sleep in his barn. It wasn't cold so it sounded like a pretty good pitch, even though the rain beat quite a tune on the tin roof.

I crawled into some hay and in a lull in the rain learned the place was full of rats. Now a few rats running round a barn are only a minor disturbance, but I soon learned there was a huge cat stalking them—all night. My sleep was really disturbed when the large cat chased a large rat across me—lengthwise.

After my wife and I had followed the outdoors for some time we went back to a California town we'd lived in, rented an apartment, and started calling old friends and inviting them over. We set up a framed tent in the living room and dragged in other stuff from our rig—cooking things, some duffle bags, and a Coleman stove. The tent looked kind of big in the middle of the room and when our old friends would show up they'd be pretty quiet.

"Oh, *that*," we'd say. "We're just used to tents and can't sleep very well without them."

It was not true.

Chapter Thirty-Four

THE
TURTLE LIFE

I f you are going to hunt and fish and tell the world about it, it is nice to have a portable camp. The trailer salesman told me how wonderful it was to carry my house with me. He said I would be just like a turtle, shielded from the elements and at home wherever I chose to stop. This was not a particularly good sales pitch as I never had much envy for turtles.

That was in the late 1940s and although there had been travel trailers and motor homes for some time, they lacked much of their present efficiency. I was about to say they have been perfected since then, but my wife just came in to report that our modern twenty-three-foot trailer, which lives in the backyard, has been leaking and a lot of paneling must be replaced. Actually, this is not all bad as it reminds me of the good old days when we were young and the fishing was always better a few hundred miles farther on.

Not everyone has pulled a thirty-four-foot trailer over the Rockies in doing more than 3,000 miles from ocean to ocean with a 1951 Oldsmobile, but when I bought the thirty-four-footer I couldn't very well use a truck for a batch of reasons. So I threw myself on the mercies of various automobile salesmen, insisting to them that I had to have power and some weight but that I was not in the luxury car bracket. I vaguely realized I needed something with considerable torque (a new word for me at the time) and, hopefully, fairly low gearing. I was chilled by the obvious lack of related knowledge on the part of various salesmen with sharp suits and large rings.

"Don't worry about power," explained one of them. "This baby will spin the wheels anywhere." I had no doubt it would do that by itself, but with the nose weight of a three-ton trailer... spinning wheels was something else. The Olds 88 I bought had horsepower all right, but a tractor it was not.

After the trailer was delivered, I had a practice session at backing and turning, doing that judiciously at midnight on the parking lot of Bay Meadows racetrack south of San Francisco. Everything went pretty well so we took the trailer on a fishing trip to northern California. I had never in my life camped in such luxury on a fishing trip, and even the trout cooperated. That was at Redding, where I also used my cartop boat for a lot of Lake Shasta bass. I even guided a few days to pay expenses.

After that, we headed toward Florida, where we intended to fish and eventually got stuck for fortysome years. It took us more than a year to get there, what with trout and pheasants along the way. I stalled out on a long mountain grade in Wyoming and made it over the top by jack-knifing and yanking in short jerks. (I have not read of this tactic in trailer manuals.) The procedure had the traffic backed up for half a mile and a wide-eyed highway patrolman wondering whether to arrest me or push the whole rig into a canyon. It was there that a helpful driver got out of his car and gave me some advice. He said it was dangerous to block traffic that way and I agreed with him. I had nothing to hit him with. The radiator was boiling and the clutch was smoking.

The mountain incident cost me the clutch, and the trip to Florida cost me almost everything else that goes into a car's suspension. We held up for a time in Denver and got jobs until we could afford to take off for Florida. Having quit a newspaper job before leaving California, I noted immediately that editors were not jostling each other to buy neatly typewritten articles about hunting and fishing. After leaving Denver, somewhere in the South we met a speeding flatbed with a sloppy load of brush. One big limb broke a trailer window and gouged a path back to the stern.

The truck with the load of brush did not stop, but we patched up the leaks and went on to a point north of New Orleans where we met some range cattle on the road on a rainy night. Along with the cattle was a pickup with six teenagers in it headed for a roller rink.

No one was hurt much but the New Orleans crash was spectacular. In passing that way later I am surprised no monument was erected to its memory, as with various Civil War battles. With the Oldsmobile rebuilt we finally made it to Florida, installed a photo lab in the trailer, and lived in it for a while. Then the publishing industry began to recognize my genius and we moved into a house, parking the trailer as a fishing camp at the edge of the saltwater Everglades on the Florida west coast. We bought a nifty little eighteen-footer for brisker travel.

As a veteran in the trailer and camper business, I wish to give readers important advice concerning map reading. Deal only in heavy lines. Never become fascinated by narrow, squiggly ones. Headed toward Michigan and some trout fishing, we followed what we thought would be a scenic route and found ourselves stuffing our car and trailer on a backcountry Ozark Mountain ferry. There had been little sign of population until we were loading, but then people appeared from all directions to see us cross. One grade-schooler admired our trailer and asked if it was paid for.

The crossing went well but there was a ditch and a slippery slope on the other side. With my wife cheering from the shoreline, I made the uphill run with a wide-open throttle and strangled steering wheel. It was a bit bumpy when I crossed the ditch and the refrigerator came open inside the trailer. We picked up our food and vowed never again to follow any map line that did not have a highway number on it. The fishing in Michigan was okay.

We decided we needed a customized van. The van craze was just getting started then. We took the van to Alaska, followed a trail somewhere in the Yukon, and met wild-eyed grayling that would eat any fly you showed them. Up to then, "muskeg" had been only a word to us. We went pretty far down into it, did some digging, and built a ramp with whatever we could cut with our ax and Swede saw. We gave thanks for the almost continuous summer daylight because we worked all night. The fishing and hunting in Alaska were pretty good.

When nobody could keep a rear wheel bearing from burning out on the van we stashed it in a garage and offered a hundred dollars to anyone who could figure what was wrong. At that time, a hundred bucks was a bunch and some technical types with strange instruments kept looking at it and measuring things, but they never figured it out and we got rid of the outfit.

Then we got a camper with almost everything you need in a house, and it was almost big enough to be called a motor home. With it and an outboard boat in tow we were pretty happy, but on the way back from a bass chasing trip in Virginia the transmission decided low gear was all we needed. That was on a big freeway through Georgia and we found a garage where they convinced us we needed a new transmission. After they put it in the speedometer showed sixty-five or better by the time we got out of second gear.

To facilitate a series of chukar chasing trips in five different western states, we really got set up—we thought. We got a nifty little thirteen-foot travel trailer and a brand new four-wheel drive, which had to be ordered. It was at a time when gasoline mileage was considered very important, and when we checked the manual on our new special-order truck we found it was not supposed to be used for any kind of towing.

The dealer said he hadn't noticed that, but that it should pull a little thirteen-foot trailer anyway. A welding shop built a complex rig to take a trailer hitch on the truck, but when we got into the mountains we went largely in second gear and the complex towing rig high-centered on almost every two-track we followed.

We've had other trailer-truck combinations that worked beautifully and therefore weren't very interesting. We've had several good-sized trailers parked at fishing sites which we sometimes didn't visit for several months. Returning after a long period was often quite exciting.

Chapter Thirty-Five

MUD, ROCKS, AND MOUNTAINS

You would have noticed Sweetwater Harry. He passed six feet early in his youth and dressed as cartoonists normally draw cowboy types—hat, big belt buckle and all, except for the boots. Instead of standard flowerpots, Sweetwater wore high-heeled packer boots with laces.

Harry and I were headed for a dressed-out elk cached in some lodgepole pines on a steeply tilted section of the Rocky Mountains. When Harry shot the elk, he said he'd "bring the jeep up here and get it." I kept quiet because I had heard a lot about Harry, though I felt privately the elk quarters were a backpacking project—or, better yet, a task for calm and tolerant pack mules.

Sweetwater Harry was a sheep rancher whose herders were scattered over mountain slopes and benches—recluses whose arks are white specks where high-grass country meets windy skies and the ragged clouds loved by western artists. A herder lived with an ark, a dog, a rifle, and a horse. Harry had to pack in occasionally to check on the herders and their flocks and to resupply them. Harry didn't use packhorses for that anymore. He checked herders, sheep, and potential sheep country with his jeep. When he went elk or deer hunting he reached camp by jeep, and although he hunted on foot his jeep carried the gear in and the meat out.

His rig had personality, if not much else. While it may seem impossible to strip down a jeep, his was. It had a cracked and taped windshield that could be straightened up for cold mornings. That was it for the trappings. I do not remember the color; maybe it was the original olive drab. I do not know if the engine was stock, but I do know that Harry was deft with tools and had the confidence of a man who could rebuild anything he used. As we left to get the elk meat, Harry somehow seemed to ride *on* instead of *in* his jeep, and it somehow seemed to have a rapport with him, having replaced those faithful mountain horses.

Harry flicked the gearshift pretty frequently, and although the shifts were smooth I wondered a little.

"I don't have any brakes," Harry said. "The brush tears everything loose, but I patch it up when I go out to the road."

For a few minutes after that I hung on pretty tightly, but I reasoned Harry had obviously been living without brakes for a long time, so I relaxed. Harry said he had no lights because the brush tore all of that stuff loose, too, but he said that in the backcountry, lights weren't much help anyway.

(At this point, I think we should cover the matter of capitalization. I don't think a World War II military jeep should have a capital J. I think one built for civilian use deserves it.)

I have here an instruction book that came with a Jeep Cherokee and explains how you should never go at an angle across a steep slope. Always go straight up, it says. That is good advice unless you do not *want* to go straight up and must go at an angle. Harry and I started across the face of a mountain. It was grassy and rocky but it wasn't muddy. We kept slipping down and it appeared that it got steeper below us. There was a great deal of mountain below us, and away down there I could look at the treetops where the slope dropped into a canyon. We were going pretty fast across the mountainside, but we kept slipping down to our right.

Finally, the rear wheels began to swing down and we were going partly sideways. We smashed into a pine tree. I jumped out and looked around. To me it had been a crash. To Harry it was another dang obstacle keeping him from his prime elk.

I don't know what I was looking for, but I figured we'd need a pry pole or something, or maybe a guardian angel or a wrecker. I heard a thud and Harry was cutting down the tree. Harry's ax was not the little survival job that came fastened to the side of the GI jeeps.

It was one of those big double-bitted numbers the real tree-fellers use in timber country. Many people have not seen a real axman at work. As the tree fell, I thought back to the fire-wood and brush I'd chopped at since childhood and realized I had never really used an ax. Maybe I had never had a really sharp ax.

Harry said not to worry about the rest of the mountainside—that there were plenty of scattered trees with which he could stop the jeep, if necessary. We went on and got the elk. A couple of days later when Harry had to go out to the highway and couldn't find the brake fluid, he used bourbon.

When a trail goes along the side of a steep hill, of course, it is a "sidle." When I became involved with Jack Ward and a group of riflemen obsessed by big mule-deer racks, we sometimes came to steep sidles where the trail was intended for mountain horses. We'd cut a good-sized pole and it would go through in such a way that some eight feet of it stuck out on the high side and a couple of us riding on it would keep the Jeep from tipping over. I have forgotten some of the details of this technique, but we never rolled Jack's rig. Jack had a metal top on his outfit—pretty plush when the November winds blew.

I have here an old photo of five really big muley bucks. At first they appear to be just a great heap of prime dressed venison lashed together by someone who knew about ropes. Look again and you'll see wheels beneath them and an expertly designed gap for a driver to peer through as he came down from the high country through deep snow with three other hunters trusting his jeep judgment.

Don't look here for gear ratios or skid-plate design. I'm no mechanic or even what they'd call an off-road hobbyist. It's just that some of us wanted to hunt and fish out back and we didn't have horses. We did have four-wheel-drive rigs that took us into surprising places, wearing their backcountry tires, often with chains all the way around. Most of us probably did some mountainside damage, but we tried not to "make roads," though it was later that the real harm of new ruts became recognized.

My wife Debie and I got one of the first of the General Motors four-wheel-drive carryalls, and although it wasn't made for tight switchbacks, we were long on power and it felt much better than a short-coupled rig after the first two thousand miles or so on the highway. In late fall, with considerable snow, Bud Schlect's usually reliable but battered and ancient Jeep quit running far back on a place called Bangtail Ridge, and Bud, Red Monical, and I walked out to the highway.

We had hunted all day when the Jeep quit and it wasn't quite all downhill coming out, but Red knew the miles to go on foot. I have never seen highway ranch lights look so friendly, but the Jeep was back in there and we had to get it out. Though I was fearful of what might happen to our treasured and shiny carryall, I took Red and Bud back in there the next day, surprised that I managed to work the big rig to where the Jeep sat looking as embarrassed as a Jeep can look and sitting in snow and half-frozen mud. I hooked on and Bud took the Jeep's wheel. For a while I hogged it along pretty smoothly, but the weather was barely freezing and the Jeep suddenly became very, very hard to tow. Its wheels had picked up freezing gumbo and all four were sliding.

Red was walking out the trail ahead—one of the best judges of traction I've ever known, even though he didn't drive automobiles himself. He said the Jeep was pulling fine except for the minor problem of the wheels not turning, so I kept going and we made it to a surfaced road. I do not blame Bud's Jeep, but the carryall was hospitalized shortly afterward. Transmission and valve troubles.

Years after four-wheel-drive had become popular in mountain and swamp country it remained quite rare in other areas, and when Debie and I were crossing the continent in one of the earliest International Scouts, we found ourselves without a clutch in a Southern town. The clutch had been a little slow in giving up but had been slipped too long in a do-or-die charge at a snowy mountain ridge.

At the twenty-four-hour truck garage the manager said there was no problem. He said he'd have it a new clutch from Memphis that night and we'd be on the road again the next morning. He then assigned a youthful employee to take us to a motel. He was a bright and pleasant kid, but I could tell something was bothering him. Finally, he blurted it out.

"Mister," he said, wide-eyed, "how fast will that thing go with all four wheels pullin'?"

The Scout was stubby and noisy, but we took it to a shop that specialized in custom work and had it upholstered and soundproofed until we could cross the country between mountains and swamps and retain a semblance of sanity.

When the Scout arrived on the scene, it was immediately compared to the jeeps and Jeeps (GI and commercial) and I began to find jeep jockeys taking me on at every opportunity. There were places where they could go and I couldn't, and it had to be a matter of traction and gear ratios as well as driving skills. (There is a little more than a heavy foot involved when the mountain is steep and high and the rocks slide or the snow slips.) With the years we had developed caution, and two rigs together was pretty standard. Then another hunter got a Scout, and for some reason he could drive happily where some of the jeeps spun out or got stuck. I decided my Scout might be a whiz on the highway, but that it wasn't up to par in the backcountry. Then, to my surprise, I found I could drive easily where a third Scout owner couldn't make it. Traction, gear ratios, weight, and weight distribution.

I went hunting with Jack Ward when our Scout was new and we followed two-tracks over a great swatch of rough country that Jack knew and I had never seen. Jack was a veteran of four-wheel-drive and he monitored my rig skeptically. Dusk was coming on as I was driving out and Jack pointed to a faint track up a very steep incline.

"Just run up that trail and we'll be able to glass the whole canyon and most of the valley," he said.

Like I said, it was a steep track, but I took a little run at it. Past some little pines my trail tipped up farther and I had the view that unstrings many a beginning off-roader—nothing but sky beyond the hood. But then we leveled off just a little and I gained some speed, listening to the uneven snarl of the little four as the wheels spun in places, and I could hear pieces of rock striking what passed for fenders. In a childish bit of driver's pride I choked the wheel harder, unwilling to have Jack learn I had broken a sweat and was pretty scared.

We reached the top suddenly, after an instant in which I saw only sky again, and I stabbed the brakes when we leveled off. Suddenly, I could see miles across a valley. We were at the very edge of a precipice and I killed the engine.

"Man, oh man!" Jack said. "I always wanted to drive up here myself but I was afraid my junker wouldn't make it!"

Nobody can accuse me of not taking advantage of a situation. I steadied my voice and said:

"Pass me the glasses, Jack. Is that a buck in that rimrock shade down there?"

Jack's been gone for some years now and I still remember how he grinned as we eased back down toward where that upward trail had petered out in a little patch of rock.

Hunters and anglers, especially hunters, used to go more frequently into steep backcountry with outfits never intended for it. I recall a nearly new Plymouth that had been abandoned some fifteen miles away from any maintained road. We saw it the summer after it had been caught in a snowstorm that closed the trails. Porcupines had eaten the tires so it must have been a bad winter up there.

There have always been adventurous souls with blind faith in their equipment, and before four-wheel-drive really invaded the automotive world, there were adventurous pilgrims who felt wheels and plenty of horsepower could conquer any space.

The road up to Montana's Gravelly Range from the Madison River valley used to be a mite primitive, but a careful driver could make it even in fairly bad weather if he had the equipment and knew his business. We were to meet a friend near the top of the Gravelly climb on the night before elk season opened one year, and we drove up there in the afternoon to set up an overnight camp just off the trail. We planted a red bandanna on a stick so our friend would know where to turn off. I had not dreamed so many hunters would come up that trail in the dark, but the local folks were after winter's meat and most of them knew the way. They drove trucks and jeeps and they knew where the handles were. There had been rain and snow and the trail was chuckholes, rock pockets, slippery patches, and mud.

Astonished at the number of rigs coming up the track, I walked over from camp just to watch. Up from the valley came the darting headlights, flicking from pine trees to boulders and grassy parks, the four-wheelers grabbing for purchase with gears whining. Part of the rigs pulled horse trailers, the savvy mountain horses with braced feet like big cats. There was the crisp rip of fast double-clutching and I stood back from the showers of mud and rock, thinking there really was some glamour to backcountry driving.

Then far down toward the valley there was a different sound. It was a scream of tortured machinery and a series of crashes and it came with lights that flicked from side to side faster than any of the others. Its tortured sound hurtled nearer—someone climbing a dark mountain with sheer velocity—and as the low black missile passed me I caught its name in a flicker of taillight—Chrysler New Yorker.

In time I learned a Great Truth. Four-wheel trouble comes most where it's least expected.

I knew about the pitfalls of tundra and bottomless muskeg and avoided them carefully in Alaska. Then I followed a new road to a grayling stream in the Yukon, pulled off on what looked like solid ground and sank. No one came along to help and we spent the night building a ramp and jacking out. Anyway, we were far enough north that there wasn't much darkness.

On a pleasant Sunday afternoon in Florida, I took my wife, pointer, and shotgun for an afternoon drive in quail country. There had been some dry years, but the rains had come and I drove slowly through several low areas where there was a little water across the road. Then I came to a deeper place and my Eagle station wagon (the first type of some years back) drowned out. When the water reached the top of the driver's seat cushion I was sure I had made an error. The old pointer sitting in the back seat and whining to start hunting said something that sounded distinctly like, "Uh-oh!" When the rig had been fished out, towed in, and partly dried out I asked my mechanic what to do next.

"Sell it," he said.

Although all of my off-road treasures have been stock or only slightly modified, I've had a sideline fascination for the real scratchers and went to watch a hill-climbing competition at Sun Valley, Idaho. While I admired the wondrous machines and their helmeted jockeys, the highlight was the realization that even the experts are fallible.

I especially admired one of the climbers that had started out as a Jeep but had acquired numerous refinements and looked like the god of horsepower. As it moved to the starting line for its run at the already churned competition slope it rumbled confidently, and with the starting signal its engine snarled viciously at the mountain.

But it went up only a little way and stalled, sliding part way back. The driver backed down to the level, cut the engine, climbed out, and unsnapped his helmet.

"I forgot to put it in four-wheel-drive," he explained.

In backcountry hunting or fishing, if you haven't been pulled out you aren't really trying. Sometimes there is a choice of puller-outers and you must remember that four-wheel drivers have their pride and some of them would rather come out with only part of your rig than admit they can't move the whole thing. From long experience, I advise it best not to ask help from drivers who wear baseball caps backward and have flames painted on the sides of their vehicles. Proud drivers of brand new outfits are poor choices for they are likely to back off as soon as they smell hot paint from their engine rooms.

At a place called Deadman we had killed some big deer, and on our last trip there we went during the muley rut when the two-track was blocked by snow. We used a shovel in a couple of places and then we climbed on foot and all deer tracks seemed to lead to a high pocket. I reached that pocket as the snow came down heavier. From a cliff I looked down upon a yard of deer, half a dozen big bucks guarding their does. Pick one and shoot. I picked one, but I did not shoot. It was only Debie and I, and a long way down there and then back to the truck, especially with a load of meat.

It was a really big buck and I hung the crosshairs of the .280 back of his shoulder. He wasn't far away, but in that snow I must have been only a shapeless blob to him. He stepped between me and one of his does and tossed his big rack.

"It's closing in," Debie warned, "probably for the winter."

So we got into the old rig and headed down the track. Even going downhill we had to shovel once as the wind whipped snow into the gaps. I can still see the big buck and all of those deer behind him. At the bottom of the descent we took off the chains and couldn't see but a few of the nearest pines back the way we had come.

There was a place beneath the Red Conglomerate Peaks on the Idaho-Montana border where we camped with the old Scout and a wall tent for several elk-season openings. It was a long and hard trail in there and the stars were very close to the little patch of aspen where we cut a single ridgepole that we used each year. Canada geese looking for a pass sometimes set their wings briefly over the little creek that went past the old tent and left us with a little high-altitude goose talk. With a spotting scope we saw bighorn sheep.

When Red Monical went in there with us, he killed a great muley buck whose head dominates any room. Once I got sick up there and Debie loaded me and the sheet-iron stove and the old tent in the Scout and brought us out. Bad flu, the doctor said.

We went back after skipping a year and I buried the old rig in a treacherous draw that had been dry before. Red Monical helped me out with a come-along, and when we made camp with the old ridgepole we found there were hunting outfits all over the hills. Unbeknownst to us, the Forest Service had built a road to our hideaway and we haven't been back, but what I remember passes pretty well for sentiment.

I thought of those times today when I got into my latest four-wheel-drive. It's fine, but there's something missing. It doesn't feel like mountains and swamps. Hell, this thing has a tilt steering wheel!